Praise for *Rethinking Your Work*

"For anyone wanting to understand innovation and enterprise, management and supervision from the heart—this is a must-read."—*Perry Kinkaide, President, Alberta Council of Technologies*

"*Rethinking Your Work* provides the reader with a wonderful prescription for having a fulfilling life at work. Skillfully weaving the personal insights of people who have spirit at work with the latest research, Dr. Kinjerski shows us the many paths to spirit at work."—*Larry Ohlhauser, MD, author,* The Healthy CEO

"This book offers a smorgasbord of simple, easy and effective ways that you can bring much more spirit into your work life. If you're wanting more nourishment for your soul at work, then this is the book for you."—*Martin Rutte, co-author,* Chicken Soup for the Soul at Work, *and Chair of the Board, Centre for Spirituality and the Workplace, Sobey School of Business, Saint Mary's University, Halifax*

"Its easy-to-read style and inspiring stories make this book a deceptively simple way for organizational leaders to introduce what could be a difficult conversation in the workplace. *Rethinking Your Work* is written by one of the key researchers in the field, and Kinjerski has field-tested all of the concepts and practices in this book and accompanying guidebook."—*Judith A. Neal, PhD, Director, Tyson Center for Faith and Spirituality in the Workplace, University of Arkansas*

"For those at a crossroad asking 'Shouldn't my work be more than just a job?' *Rethinking Your Work* guides readers to not only become their own change agent but also an agent of change in building an environment which honours 'the heart of what matters' to all who seek to live a values-based life at work."—*Barb Gardner, MA, Educator, SAIT Polytechnic*

"As a foremost authority, Dr. Kinjerski has condensed almost 10 years of research and experience into an eminently readable text filled with stories and pragmatic advice. *Rethinking Your Work* shows how anyone can find spirit at work by getting to the heart of what matters."—*Lance Secretan, founder, Secretan Center, and best-selling author of* ONE: The Art and Practice of Conscious Leadership

"*Rethinking your Work* is definitely a page-turner. I am impressed with the timeliness of the concepts in today's labour market."
—*Cindy Ruzycki, Academic Advisor, Red Deer College, Alberta*

"As a human resources professional, this is a book I would highly recommend to fellow HR practitioners and management. If you have ever wondered why some individuals seem so energized and engaged at work while others appear to be putting in time, this book will enlighten you!"
—*Kellie Auld, CHRP, Human Resources Advisor*

"Val's book is a must for anyone who wants to lead a more purposeful life both at work and at home. The thought-provoking questions and exercises encourage people to grow both professionally and personally and to fully understand how they can choose to make a difference at work every single day. It will touch minds and hearts so that any reader will be challenged to be the very best he or she can be. Thank you, Val, for inspiring us to rethink what we do every day!"—*Barbara Glanz, professional speaker and author,* The Simple Truths of Service Inspired by Johnny the Bagger® *and* CARE Packages for the Workplace

"*Rethinking Your Work* is an inspiring book for people to gain more clarity and trust with what they really want and need in their work and personal lives. . . . This book is an extremely valuable tool full of opportunities to reflect on living with purpose."—*Jacqui Sample, CHRP, Executive Director, Strategic Enterprise Transformation, Deputy City Manager's Office, Edmonton*

"This is a book I will definitely purchase and give as gifts to the people I love. It is filled with gems such as asking yourself, 'Where is the poetry in my day?' to 'What would I do if I were ten times bolder?' It is not just another self-help book; it is a self-heal book written with compassion and grace."
—*Olive Yonge, RN, PhD, RPsych, Professor and Vice-Provost (Academic Programs), University of Alberta*

"*Rethinking Your Work* gets you to look at what's really important to you and provides you with a hands-on approach . . . to find out where your passion truly is. . . . Outstanding!"—*Lori-Ann Muenzer, Olympic gold medalist, motivational speaker and author*

Rethinking Your Work

Getting to the Heart of What Matters

Val Kinjerski, PhD

Kaizen Publishing

This book is dedicated to my husband,
Fred Shaughnessy,
With love and gratitude.

Cover and Interior Design: Lara Shecter, Bodega Books
Editing: Pam Withers
Proofreading: Naomi Pauls, Paper Trail Publishing

Library and Archives Canada Cataloguing in Publication

Kinjerski, Val, 1955–

Rethinking your work : getting to the heart of what matters / Val Kinjerski

Includes bibliographical references.

ISBN 978-0-9812122-0-3

1. Quality of work life. 2. Job satisfaction. 3. Positive psychology.
4. Self-actualization (Psychology). I. Title.

HD6955.K54 2009   650.1   C2009-904126-X

Discounts on bulk quantities for Kaizen books are available to corporations, professional associations, educational institutions and other organizations. For details and discount information, visit our website at www.rethinkingyourwork.com.

Published 2009. Printed and bound in Canada.
13 12 11 10 09   1 2 3 4 5
Published by Kaizen Publishing
www.rethinkingyourwork.com
info@rethinkingyourwork.com

Contents

Acknowledgments

ppreciation and gratitude are key elements of spirit at work, and I have many people I would like to thank. Unaware of others exploring what I came to call "spirit at work," I knew that I was on the right track when I stumbled across a book by Lance Secretan. *Reclaiming Higher Ground: Creating Organizations that Inspire the Soul* gave me the courage to study spirit at work: what it is and how to create it.

When I decided to research and complete a doctorate in the area of spirit at work, I was extremely fortunate to find an advisor, Dr. Berna Skrypnek, who fully embraced the topic. She quickly went from being an advisor to being a friend and colleague. Together we developed the spirit-at-work scale and tested the spirit-at-work program. Berna, your excitement and enthusiasm about my work never waned. Thank you for your unconditional support.

Rethinking Your Work and the *Rethinking Your Work Guidebook* never would have come about without the people who agreed to tell me their stories and participate in my research. Many of you spent hours with me and for this I am most grateful. Because some of you asked not to be identified, I agreed to use pseudonyms rather than real names for everyone. A special thanks to the real Ben, Betty, Bill, Bob, Don, Donna, Frank, Harry, Hashim, Hien, Jason, Jim, Karla, Kelly, Ken, Kevin, Lana, Larry, Maureen, Mike, Molly, Monica, Myron, Neal, Noreen, Paul, Phil, Rose, Rowena, Sandra, Sheila, Sue and Vivian. Further thanks to all of you who shared your story while we shared space and time on a plane, in a meeting, at a conference or in a taxi. I am sorry that I do not have your name and cannot properly acknowledge you.

Thank you also to each of you who attended my keynote addresses and workshops and who have been so generous with sharing your stories and providing feedback about the exercises and spirit-at-work program. It was through these workshops and your feedback that I tested and perfected the exercises.

After hearing all of these wonderful stories and designing and testing a program to create spirit at work, I came to a point in my writing of *not* writing. I was doing a lot of talking about writing a book but wasn't putting anything down on paper. I knew that I either needed to find a way to complete it or let it go. Yet I also knew that letting it go wasn't an answer. This book wasn't *about* me and it wasn't *for* me. I was being pulled along to share what I knew to be a profoundly new way to be in the workplace. Through the Canadian Association of Professional Speakers (CAPS), I launched the CAPS Writer's Group which became my way to complete the book. While the membership has changed over time, our purpose remains the same: to support one another in our writing. Thank you for being there.

How naïve I was to think that the book was complete once I had finished writing. There are so many other, behind-the-scenes craftspeople who help bring a book to print. Thank you to Charmaine Hammond and Katherine Weinmann, who both stopped their world just before Christmas to read and provide feedback on *Rethinking Your Work*. Thank you to Pam Withers for your highly skilled and efficient editing abilities. I have never met such a fast editor! Naomi Pauls of Paper Trail Publishing is a proofreader extraordinaire. Your support went well beyond the realm of proofreading. Lara Shecter of Bodega Books is the only graphic designer I know who reads a book before she designs it — and it shows. Thank you.

I have been blessed with a loving family who never seem to tire of my stories and my commitment to my work. Thank you to my mom and dad, Lill and Mike, who have shown me that there is more to work than a paycheck. I wish my dad were still with us to see his influence. My brother Phil continues to be an inspiration. You are something else.

Joey, you continue to teach me that which I am teaching others. As early as grade four, you were able to point out spirit at work. You are the most authentic, caring person I know. Thank you for being my son.

Finally, a special thanks to my husband and soul mate, Fred Shaughnessy. You have been my greatest fan and supporter. Many times you have set aside your work to review yet another chapter, help me choose the right editor, view another layout or simply listen. I can do a lot of things, but I do not think I would have written this book without you. Thank you.

Introduction

Can you imagine . . . looking forward to work every day? Being passionate about your work? Knowing that you make a difference and feeling good about the work you do? This is the experience of people who have spirit at work. This is what is possible by simply rethinking work.

There is more to work than putting in eight, ten or twelve hours a day. Work is much more than meeting deadlines and coming in under budget. And there is definitely more to work than a paycheck and pension. Money isn't everything and it certainly doesn't buy the fulfillment many of us are seeking. Yes, we need money to put a roof over our head and food on the table, but once we have that, most of us find we are looking for more. That "more" is an opportunity to make the world a better place. To do meaningful work and make a difference in the lives of others. To feel good about what we are doing. To have spirit at work.

Spirit at work is present in people who are passionate about and energized by their work. These are the people who would continue to work even if they won a lottery, because to them, work is an opportunity to make a contribution. Spirit at work is something that is inside each person. Accessing it is an inside job.

We can all have spirit at work. Take Ken. As a parking lot attendant, he enjoys spirit at work. He has found a way to make a difference in the lives of others.

Ken works in a tiny booth in an underground parkade near a medical center. At first glance, it appears that Ken just takes people's money and hands out parking passes. On closer inspection, he does much more than that. Ken has spirit at work. He sees the parking lot as an extension of himself, so he often sweeps the entrance to the parkade, picks up garbage and cleans the windows of his booth. He says he would not have you come to his home if it looked like a pigsty, so why would he have you come to a dirty parkade?

When assigned to this particular site, Ken decided to get to know the people who parked in "his parkade." Some were regulars who worked in the building, whereas others were parents bringing their children in for medical appointments. As they came through, he would offer each person a smile, get to know them by name and share a few words. He became curious about the people coming through on a daily basis and began to ask about them, their family and their work. At first, he received strange looks. People did not know how to respond. But soon, he was on a first-name basis with all his regulars.

Because the parkade is off the beaten track, it had a high vacancy rate when Ken first arrived. It didn't take long, however, before the "parkade full" sign lit up on a regular basis. People told him they went out of their way to use his parkade, often passing other parking lots. They looked forward to that positive thirty-second conversation.

Ken was troubled by all the children coming for medical appointments and wanted to do something to brighten their day. He decided to buy and pass out candies to each child coming through the parkade. He was very careful not to miss any children sleeping in the backseat. When he ran short on candies, he slipped out during his break to the nearest drugstore to replenish his stock until he could get to a discount store and buy a larger supply. He purchased the candies with his own money, saying that it cost little to bring such happiness.

Mothers came out of their way to thank him for his kindness. It turned out that most of these children resisted coming for the appointments until their parents, mostly mothers, assured them, "That nice man with the candies is going to be there." Mothers who felt badly about exposing their children to invasive medical procedures were very grateful.

Ken has spirit at work. Spirit at work is about finding meaning and fulfillment in one's job. It is about making a contribution, a difference — and in doing so, feeling good. Ken's deeper meaning and fulfillment comes from making a difference in the lives of his customers. Putting a smile on the face of the children. Hearing that drivers go out of their way to have contact with him. His eyes fill with tears as he relates the stories of mothers expressing their appreciation. It is clear that Ken sees his work as an act of service and that his work is about serving the customer, not about him.

When we have spirit at work, we enjoy a sense of alignment between what is important to us and the work we do. When we are in alignment, there is a match between our work and our deeper purpose, and that leads to a sense of well-being. Ken's deeper purpose is to make people happy, so it doesn't really matter where he works. What matters is how he works and how he thinks about his work. His boss calls him the "ambassador" because he greets everyone he meets and makes them feel welcome. To him, the parkade is just a stage on which he can act and bring joy to others.

· · · · · · ·

Not everyone enjoys spirit at work like Ken. When I was a senior manager and later a consultant, I saw many people struggling with stress and burnout, while others described their work as meaningful, a way to make a contribution and gain personal fulfillment. I became curious about how those struggling with stress or burnout differed from those who were passionate about their work. I named this phenomenon of having passion for what you do "spirit at work" because there seemed to be an energy — a life force — that inspired these people despite challenges.

This curiosity moved me to return to university to complete a PhD that involved researching spirit at work. I was privileged to interview several people like Ken who enjoy spirit at work. Based on their stories about how they cultivate and maintain that spirit, I developed workshops and a spirit-at-work program. Although the workshop evaluations were very positive, I always wondered whether the workshops had any lasting effect. When the opportunity arose to test the impact of the spirit-at-work program, I jumped at it. Before and after participating in the program, a team of health care workers completed several questionnaires about spirit at work, work attitudes and well-being. At the end of the program, they took part in focus groups. Finally, I examined absenteeism and turnover rates for the team prior to and after the program. I compared the results of these efforts with a similar team that did not participate in the program.

Much to my delight, I found that not only did participants' spirit at work increase, so did their job satisfaction and commitment to the organization. They felt good about their work and the contribution they were making. They looked forward to going to work.

When teams took the program together, the organizational culture strengthened, especially teamwork and morale. They saw an improvement in communication and relationships. Stress decreased. Not surprisingly, absenteeism and turnover also dropped significantly for all employees who participated in the program.

When I first started to research spirit at work, people assumed it was an experience for an elite group — professionals like teachers, doctors, nurses and social workers who chose their profession because they wanted to help others. And yes, I did interview people in these careers who had spirit at work. But, like you, I am aware of many people in the helping fields who are struggling with stress and burnout. For them, spirit at work seems to be the impossible dream.

I also met people who took a job because they needed work in order to pay the bills and the position was available. The parking lot attendant, the taxi driver, the real estate agent, the administrative assistant — they didn't dream of doing this work. It wasn't something they had always hoped to do. Ken was looking for work and saw a want ad for a parking lot attendant. He applied and got the position. Rose wanted an excuse to get out of her house and social obligations and saw an advertisement for a real estate agent. She liked houses, so decided to apply.

When Hashim couldn't find work in his profession, he looked around to see what he could do to earn a living that would support his family. Many friends and family members in the same predicament were driving taxi, so he thought he would give it a try. Relationships were important to Sheila, so she looked for a job where she could work with others. Even though Ken, Rose, Hashim and Sheila did not start out being passionate about their work, they all got to the point where they loved the work they were doing.

Spirit at work is available to us regardless of gender, age or education level. It doesn't matter if we are a blue-collar worker, a professional or self-employed. It doesn't matter whether we get paid for our work. We can all have spirit at work. We can all feel inspired by what we do. We just need to take steps to create that feeling.

For some of us, spirit at work is about following our passion. For others, following a passion is not enough. We only have to look at the number of nurses, teachers and social workers who leave their chosen field after a few years, disenchanted.

People who follow their passion can also lose their way. Once we lose touch with why we are doing the work we do and how it makes a difference, all the constraints, pressures and lack of resources can feel overwhelming. So how can we expect to feel good about our work, never mind experience spirit at work?

Perhaps you have lost touch with what first drew you to your particular work. Maybe you took your job because you needed work and never took the opportunity to uncover the deeper meaning of what you do each day. You might be at a time in your life where work feels like an unsatisfying burden. Family and personal responsibilities may require you to stay in your current job. Perhaps you will retire in a few years and want to leave your work in a good way — feeling good about your organization and your contribution.

I have found that there are two ways to get to spirit at work: Discover and follow your passion, or find the deeper meaning in your current work. Do what you love or love what you do. That's what inspired me to write this book and share the stories of how everyday people come to have spirit at work. From their experiences, I have created and tested a process you can follow to bring forth or enhance your spirit at work.

• • • • • • •

We are co-creators of our lives and our work experiences. *Rethinking Your Work* is about finding spirit at work simply by becoming clear about what is important to us and by thinking about our work differently. The power lies within each of us. Yet too often we give away our power. We wait for someone to make things better. "If only the people in this company understood what I am up against and showed that they cared. If only the president would provide more resources. If only this government would appreciate clients' needs. If only I could hire more staff. . ." You get the point. Not that these aren't valid concerns. The only problem we face with "if only" is that we give away our power. And when we give away our power, we are left waiting for someone else to take care of the situation. In the meantime, we become disillusioned, disenchanted and disengaged.

Rethinking Your Work will start you on a life-altering process that inspires and guides the creation of spirit at work. Through the stories and experiences of real people who have spirit at work, you will learn the personal actions and strategies that foster it. Completing exercises tested through workshops and the spirit-at-work program will help you regain your power to create spirit at work.

· · · · · · · ·

This book is divided into two parts. In the first part, you will meet people like yourself who now enjoy spirit at work. (Although their stories are real, I have changed their names in order to maintain confidentiality.) These stories will illustrate what spirit at work is and the different paths one might take to get to spirit at work. The second part focuses on transformative actions that will lead to spirit at work. Here you will learn what people did to create and maintain their spirit at work, how to appreciate yourself and others, how to live purposefully and consciously, how to cultivate a spiritual, values-based life and how to refill your cup. The exercises and reflections will show how you make a difference through your work, something we all do whether we're aware of it or not, and will help you uncover your spirit at work.

Rethinking Your Work provides a process and tools to discover your spirit at work. The exercises in this book and companion guidebook — *Rethinking Your Work Guidebook: How to Get to the Heart of What Matters* — will help you go inside yourself and get in touch with what really matters to you. Some of the exercises ask you to reflect on your personal life and others direct themselves to your work experiences. Both help you get to the heart of what matters and ensure that you learn how to bring more of that into your life and work. They will lead to a rethinking of your work. Exercises in the companion guidebook are identified by this symbol: ▯

You can begin *Rethinking Your Work* wherever you like. If you need further understanding about spirit at work or some inspiration to get started on your own path, start at the beginning. If you already feel inspired and want to get at it, skip to the second part and begin working. Either way, expect to notice a difference in how you think and feel about your work. Although a few people choose to change jobs, most people find spirit at work by learning to love their existing job. By looking at their work differently, they uncover the deeper meaning in their current work and begin to engage in personal practices that bring joy and spirit into it. Everything changes when we rethink our work. Guaranteed.

Reflection Questions

1. What was it about this book that attracted your attention?
2. What do you hope to gain from reading it?
3. What is the one thing that will make reading this book worthwhile?
4. What is one thing you can do to increase the possibility of that happening?
5. How open are you to a new way of thinking about work?
6. Are you open to the experience of spirit at work?

PART I

UNDERSTANDING SPIRIT AT WORK

chapter one

Stories from the Workplace

I find that the best way to understand spirit at work is by example. The following stories come from people who participated in my research and shared their story so that others could learn to enjoy work.

You met Ken in the introduction. People drove blocks out of their way to be able to park in Ken's parkade. There is just something about being in the presence of people who experience spirit at work. As you read these stories, I suspect that you will be thinking:

- How can I get my teenager into that teacher's class?
- Are there truly real estate agents that care that much?
- I sure hope that when my parents get sick they will have caring nurses.
- I would love to have her for a hairdresser!
- Society would be very different if we had more police like this.
- This is the landscape designer I want designing my yard.
- It would be a privilege to call this person my doctor.
- That mother and son were graced by the social worker's presence.
- I bet that dentist can sing.

- Can you imagine what university would be like if all professors planted seeds?
- Sign me up.

VIVIAN

The Making of a Teacher

I didn't even know that I wanted to be a teacher. When I was eighteen or nineteen years old, like most students finishing high school, I was lost. I didn't know what to do. My brother, a school counselor, said, "I think you should go into education. I totally see you there. You care about people so much." And for me, that is the main thing. I like to be around people. So not knowing what else to do, I went to university to become a teacher.

I didn't really know what I was doing, but when I started my field practicum, that was it! I knew that teaching was for me. I was surrounded by people who needed me and I felt like I could make a difference. I could help them change something in their lives. Later I knew that I wanted to build on that.

I know that I am doing what I love. I am here because I want to teach. I love planning the lessons, and when I get into class and see my students' reactions to what I prepared for them, that is what gives me the feeling that my work is the best. When the students are present and I know they are listening to me — well, that just gives me more passion. And I feel that if I am passionate about what I am teaching, they will be passionate about learning. They will love it like I do and so they will listen to me and get the information they need. Sometimes I feel that even if my lesson is not the best lesson, I make a difference. I know that it is the relationship I have with these students that counts.

These kids are amazing people and I know that they will do great things in life. I am also very aware that fourteen- and fifteen-year-olds do not want to be controlled. So I say to them, "I am not here to tell you what to do. I am not here to be superior to you. I am here to care about you. I am here to love you and teach you because that is my job. We are all at the same level. There are areas that you know more than me and there are areas that I know more than you." I respect them and they respect me back. When you show students respect and treat them fairly, you can get them to do anything.

I have a really hard time seeing students who are bored. That just breaks my heart. So when I see that, I have to get them involved. I have to get them to understand. And when they do understand, it feels so good. This year, because of the group of students I had and the challenges they brought to the classroom, I had to work harder, much harder. I am surprised, though, that I had way more fun and I enjoyed my job even more. I think it is because of the results I am getting. Because I am passionate, I spend extra effort to reach these students. They become engaged and they enjoy my class even more. So they are having fun and I am also having fun.

My job is more than a matter of me giving. I feel like my students are giving me as much, if not more, than I give. They give me so much energy. I am not looking for anything back, but I do get it and it feels so good. I feel like this every day!

ROSE

Real Estate Is What Makes Her Tick

Real estate is what makes me tick. It makes me want to get up in the morning. When I wake up, I can't wait to get out of bed. I enjoy people and feel that I am doing something helpful. When I was a buyer of china, it was great. I loved it. I love china. My house is full of it. I loved the people there, but I wasn't giving the same service as I am now. I feel that this is a very good service I can give people, and when I see how much they appreciate it, it makes me want to work a little harder and be a little better at it.

I feel good that I am able to help people out. If they are being transferred, it is always very traumatic for them to take their kids out of school, pack up and leave their homes. So I do whatever I can to make it easier for them. I get them information about the city they are moving to: schools, maps, services, whatever they need. I know one or two realtors in every office, so I always phone ahead and tell them about the people who are coming. I just keep right on helping them until they are on their way. I have even driven some clients to the airport.

For clients who stay in the city, I would never just sell a house and forget about them. Starting around October, I make a couple of hundred jars of antipasto and Christmas marmalade, and I get my son, who owns a flower shop, to put these items in a big basket with a poinsettia. Then

I take them around to my clients. This is my way of saying thanks, and they are so appreciative. When people buy a house, the agent usually receives several thousand dollars in commission. To me, it seems like too much if the relationship ends there. Of course, providing extra value is good business, too. When they are happy with my services, they pass my name on. But I love doing things for people. When they have faith in me and they appreciate what I have done, I think it is worthwhile. I just love it. I just love doing it.

Over the years, many clients have become my friends. Seven or eight years ago, I would make a dozen muffins every Friday night. Then on Saturday morning, I would take them around to different clients whose homes I had sold — just as a little gift. Maybe they were alone or in a nursing home. It was something for them to look forward to. But then the number got bigger and bigger and I was making up to eighteen muffins. Sometimes I didn't have time on a Friday night to make them, so I convinced a tea shop to make them for me. It started at twenty; now it has increased to anywhere between fifty and fifty-four. I deliver Saturday mornings. So when people ask me if I can come and look at their house, I say, "Not before noon, because I have to deliver my muffins." So they call me the muffin lady.

KELLY

An ICU Nurse Is Guided to Save Her Patient

This experience will probably be with me until my dying breath. I was twenty-four years old and working as a nurse in the intensive care unit (ICU) in a small northern city. That evening, I was working the night shift — from midnight to eight in the morning. It was only a four-bed ICU, so I was on shift by myself. My only patient was a gentleman who had been admitted earlier in the evening with a coronary, a myocardial infarction (heart attack). He wasn't doing very well.

There wasn't much I could do, but I felt a strong pull to be with this man and to hold his hand. The pull was so strong that I felt like I was being guided. After I got the information from the nurse who was on shift before me, I went to his bedside, sat down and took his hand. As soon as I held his hand, I could feel the energy moving from me to him and it wasn't my energy — I was just a conduit. I held his hand all night. Unless I had to do other things like take his blood pressure or give medications,

I was at his side holding his hand. I balanced the chart on my knees, making notes as I held his hand. I was rarely away from him for that eight-hour period. I knew that I had to do that; otherwise he would die.

Come morning, the nurses on shift knew that they wouldn't find me behind the desk, so they came to find me by the patient's bed. They were used to me and knew that I never took breaks at night except to go to the washroom. I shared information with them, but of course didn't say anything about being guided to hold the patient's hand throughout the night. Those are the stories that we tell only rarely. I thought, "Okay, that is between me and the guy or the gal upstairs."

When I came back to work a couple of days later, the patient was still there. He was much improved and just about ready to be transferred to the medical unit. He looked at me and said, "You are the reason I am still here." I got goose bumps and said, "Tell me more about that." To which he said, "You stayed with me that first night."

I was shocked. He was hardly conscious that night, so I am not sure how he knew. Most people don't remember anything about what happens when they first go into an ICU. They tend to be out of it and wake up maybe three days later. It is only then that they become aware of what is happening. So that was unusual.

Two or three months later, I was walking down the street when I ran into him and his wife. Because I mostly worked nights, I hadn't seen his wife much during his illness and didn't recognize her. As soon as he saw me, he came right up to me and introduced me to his wife and said, "This nurse is the reason I am still here." And I knew that to be true.

MAUREEN

A Hairdresser's Scissors Seem to Cut on Their Own

I knew as a little girl that I wanted to be a hairdresser. As far back as I could remember, I was always playing with people's hair. My Uncle Alby had only two strands of hair across the top of his head, but I would still tie bows in it. So I decided early on that I was going to be either a hairdresser or a singer, and for a while, I did both. I left school just after my sixteenth birthday and began an apprenticeship program. I came from a working-class family, but I wanted something glamorous. To me, hairdressing and singing were both glamorous. In the end, hairdressing won out.

Arriving at spirit at work has been quite a journey. I have been a hairdresser for twenty-six years and, let me tell you, it has not always been easy. I have had real ups and downs. My marriage fell apart. I went back to England for a couple of years to do music, so when I came back I had to build up my hairdressing clientele again. The company I was working for went under and I lost a month's wages, so I had to start all over again. Then the next company went under, too. It has been a real roller coaster ride.

But this is my forty-second year and it is my best year. It is just like — I am so into it. You know, I feel really complete. I was just a late bloomer, I guess. I feel a lot calmer now; this is the best it has been, for sure. But if I hadn't had those lows of losing my job and month's worth of lost wages a couple of times — and then going back to England and having a tough time there and coming back here — if I hadn't gone that low, I couldn't have gotten to where I am now. I think that is a lot of it; it was just a complete journey.

I am a really giving person and I really value that. I feel like I have a lot to give to people. I have really great clients and we have great conversations. Some clients have been with me for twenty years, and I really value our relationship. I had one client say, "Oh, I am so sorry, dear, but you are the only person that I can talk to." And I feel good that I could be that important in somebody's life. You don't realize that maybe you are doing more for them than just cutting their hair. I don't mind that, because I am impartial. I'm not related to them; I don't judge them. I just listen and if they want suggestions, then I will do that, but I tend not to. There is a lot of spirit at work in your relations with people. I love what I do and I think I am good at it. I really get a lot out of styling hair. I like that it is a creative job and it is always changing. I just really enjoy it, even after twenty-six years, and I enjoy it right now more than I ever have.

To me, a good day is when everything comes together. Everything clicks. You have great clients coming in, and you can even deal with the ones that are a little more high-maintenance because you are in the zone. Everything is going well. For instance, when I give somebody a head massage, it completely relaxes me. I just feel really zoned in. I get all starry and feel like, "This is really good." I really enjoy doing that to somebody. It is a real energy. That is the only way I can describe it. It is just a real big energy level and I really feel like I am in that zone. I could do just anything and it would be perfect.

I get days when I think, "God, my haircuts are *great* today." I know they are always good, but sometimes they are just great! Everything is just clicking; the conversation is great. It is almost like the scissors are moving by themselves. It is as if this other energy is just working through me. It feels like it would be hard to do anything wrong, and I am surprised if something goes wrong on one of these days. It is at that point that I think, "Hey, I've arrived."

Achieving spirit at work wasn't as big an arrival as I thought it would be, but you know, it was like my life began at a very late age. It felt right and good and exciting.

SANDRA

How a Police Officer Helps

I like people and I like helping them. That is what I love. And no matter what I am doing in my work, I know that I am helping them. Even if it is a bad situation and I am fighting with them or I am forcing them into the police car, I am still helping someone who has been hurt or might be hurt by that person. Maybe I am helping the person from hurting himself or from whatever he is doing, like driving impaired. What if he went around the corner and killed someone else or died himself? I think about the person and those attached to him or her. He has a mother, a father, a brother, a sister and an extended family. I think about the impact on them.

So I want to make sure that I am helpful. I don't care if they are yelling and swearing and screaming at me; I still think I am helping, even if they don't realize it. Even if they don't want me to be there, because most of them don't. No matter who they are or what they are doing, I should help them. That's all; that is what I like.

The most rewarding case I worked on was a sexual assault investigation that was open for nearly eight months. The father was convicted of sexually assaulting his two young daughters and one of their friends and was sent to jail for almost six years. I became very connected to these girls. I took statements from them and I visited them often at their house before court dates. Even though it wasn't always easy, I was happy to be the one talking to the girls because I knew that they would remember this for the rest of their lives. So I would rather it be somebody really sensitive about the situation and able to help them through it, than someone who might make it worse than it really was. I was able to do that. So it made me feel good to be part of someone's bad experience which was a big part of their life. Sexual assault is not something you want any child to go through or remember. But they are going to remember it, so you want the contact with the police and court to be as positive as possible.

Two months after the court case was over, both girls came to the office to see me. They each wrote me letters, thanking me and saying things like, "Your smile made me comfortable." The older girl still calls me. She will call me at work and say things like, "I just want to ask you about this feeling I am having." It was almost two years ago I worked on that case. I know she has a big connection with me. It is a huge thing for someone to share their experience about a sexual assault. It is just that person and me in a room, and she is telling me, a stranger, the most secretive and probably most painful thing in her life. There are lots of rewarding times in this work, but that was a very rewarding moment and it continues to be every time I talk with her. And getting their thank-you letters made up for all the other people who never think about thanking a police officer. Even though it is nice to be acknowledged and to hear that you helped someone, I am not doing this work to be thanked or recognized. I am doing it because I love people and I want to make a difference. I feel like I do that every day.

KARLA

A Landscape Designer's Passion

As a landscape designer I work on design projects. I become so engaged with the visualization that I block other things out and often get totally lost in the project. I am looking at this and that possibility and what they would be like in combination. I love the problem solving involved, because I have to meet certain needs and I have to fit things in a certain area. If somebody wants a deck, hot tub and patio, it all has to fit, so I am problem solving in terms of spatial relationships.

I am also thinking about the individual in terms of customizing — creating fresh ideas, and maybe creating something that is a hook. For example, one person for whom I am completing a design is interested in art and does landscape painting. So I am thinking about how to bring art into her garden. Where am I going to create an art wall or a walk she can stroll along where art — maybe statues — are on display?

Then I have to think about how to make this look good and visualize how it is going to look from each angle. Standing here, how is it going to look? How about from over there? If I put a tree here, what is it going to do? So I find that process really engaging. I am so completely into it that I don't notice the time. I am not really thinking about the time; I am not really thinking of anything else. I am quite full of the work itself. And that happens regularly.

So my passion comes out as ideas. I keep looking to find an idea that will make the whole design flow and represent who my client is. All of a sudden, I realize this is it. I have the key idea. This is going to work. Now I have to make sure we have a little patio area besides that, and a pathway coming off of that going somewhere else. And the design becomes complete and I am fulfilled. So my spirit at work comes from being engaged, being creative and finding artistic solutions to my clients' problems.

DONNA

The Privilege of a Physician

There have been so many times I have been aware of my spirit at work. I have tremendous rewards in my work. Treating acutely ill people who are not expected to come back, and they do. When I make the right diagnosis. When I see somebody get better with the treatment I offer. The patient gets their own pleasure with getting to feel better, but I almost feel a guilty pleasure that I get to enjoy that as well, and other people in the world don't.

My work is not always joyful. Unexpected things happen. Sometimes, the outcomes are not good, but I am able to help the patient and their family come to terms with and accept the bad news. Being there with them. I have seen some patients look so desperate and so frightened, and sometimes all I can do is say, "I will go through this with you. I will be there." And I see them relax just a little. It is still scary and often devastating — losing a limb, losing a child, losing their life, whatever it is — but they know they will not be alone.

Sometimes the day doesn't end. So in the middle of the night, I might find myself doing a difficult delivery, where the heart rate is falling and everybody is starting to sweat. I put on those forceps and they glide on and I extract a baby that is still in good health that, otherwise, was going to be compromised. Personally, I find that gives me a tremendous sense of satisfaction and reward, seeing the glow in the parents' faces and seeing everybody in the maternity case room relax. That business of maternity is a risky business, even when you think that it is not going to be. It can surprise you at the end.

On days when I am exhausted or have had a bad outcome or been particularly humbled, I do have to ask myself, "Why am I doing this?" I know that my work gets in the way of my health, it gets in the way of time with my family, it gets in the way of learning more, and it gets in the way of having balance and holidays and getting on the treadmill. Sure it gets in the way of a lot. Apparently not enough. I know that I have to do this. There is something in me that will not be satisfied and I won't be fun to live with if I don't do it.

I do this because people suffer less as a result of the care I have given them. There are enough positive times to outweigh the bad times. And because I like this science. Of all the sciences, I like this science — the science of the human body. And there is always something new going on.

In addition to making a difference in the lives of others, I wanted to do something where there would always be a learning process. And I have both. So why shouldn't I get up and go to work the next day? Every day, I get the privilege of doing this work because of the training and experience I have. It is overwhelmingly positive. Overwhelmingly. Like not just a little. Overwhelmingly.

MONICA

The Gift to a Social Worker

I was a social worker doing community outreach in an aboriginal school. One day I was assigned to work with a teenage boy who was very depressed and suicidal. This boy was a big kid. He was tall and heavy for his age and was struggling with constantly being teased. He wasn't doing well in school and spent a lot of time at home, alone. His mother seemed to be oblivious to his needs. She, too, was struggling. As a single parent, it took all she had to make a living and support her family. At the end of the day, it seemed like she had nothing left.

I worked closely with the teacher and psychologist to support this young man. I also worked with his mom to help her understand the seriousness of her son's needs and guided her to support him through this difficult time. He desperately needed attention and to have his feelings validated. I was able to do that and help his mom understand that, too.

In this particular situation, the boy and his mom responded very quickly. Sometimes it doesn't take much. Sometimes these kids just need to be listened to. To be cared for and loved. That mom found it within herself to give her son the affection and sense of belonging that he needed. I knew that I'd made a difference for both the boy and his mom. What I didn't know was whether the effects would last.

Much to my surprise, this young man and his mother tracked me down a few years later to say thanks and to let me know how well he was doing. They are still very connected and supportive of each other. Today this young man is using his size to his advantage; he provides security at concerts.

I was overwhelmed to think they took the time to find me. This feedback just doesn't happen, especially in child protection. It was an amazing feeling — one of the highlights of my career. It is experiences like this that keep me going and help me maintain my spirit at work, especially during the times that I am not so sure whether I am having an impact.

LARRY

A Dentist Feels Like a Singer Who Can Hit the High Notes

You asked about a time that I felt most alive, most involved and most excited about my work, and I would have to say that I feel like this every day. We are not like doctors who actually save lives, but we do get people who are very emotionally upset. There are times when we help someone who is in desperate pain when they come in and they leave feeling so relieved. The feeling is one of just total satisfaction, like I *really, really* helped someone. And when I do that, I have this feeling that what I have and what I give to someone is really above everything. It feels very spiritual.

We care about our patients and I know that we make a positive difference in their lives. For example, we have always acknowledged our patients, and at one point we decided to send them birthday cards. One of my patients is a young lady probably twenty to twenty-five years old and has some mental challenges. When she got a birthday card from us, she was so moved by our kindness that she immediately phoned the dental office. Crying, she said that that was the only birthday card she had ever received in her whole life. Situations like this stand out.

To me, I am not just doing what I am doing in the mouth. I am dealing with people's feelings and their mind and well-being. Patients have said to me, "Tell me when you are retiring so I can have my teeth pulled and get dentures so that I don't have to see anyone else." I guess it is these comments that tell you that your patients are happy with you.

I think I feel like a singer who can hit those high notes and people applaud. I can't sing, I can't draw, I can't sculpt, I can't fix machines, but boy, can I fix teeth and help people. And that feeling, of the gift I have been given and how I am using it, is what helps me enjoy spirit at work every day.

ROWENA

A Professor Plants Seeds

Last Friday I was giving a presentation at a teachers' conference. My talk was on stem-cell research and the conflict between science and religion. Lots of science teachers, lots of religion teachers and many interested others attended. There was a sense of curiosity for many of them. They were looking for a different level of knowledge and expertise, which, yes, I could offer. However, that was not *all* I felt I could offer. I felt that I was helping them see and recognize, and then become trained themselves in engaging in that kind of dialogue, where it is potentially so divisive.

Considering such strong and opposing views such as those held about stem-cell research, how can we actually bring these people to the table with respect? Because above all, the main outcome is respect for each other's human dignity, no matter how extreme they might be on either side. And I witnessed that happening in my session.

I think teachers are searching for ways to do this in their classrooms as well. Often, high school students see these issues in shades of black and white. Some, if they are more advanced, see shades of gray. So, how do you help students explore ethical issues while honoring each other's values and views and showing respect? How do you facilitate that dialogue?

Afterwards, many came up to me and thanked me for being able to show them how to do that. Having experienced it themselves, they felt they were going to be able to use these skills in discussions with their high school students. It was just great to see that they got what they were looking for and reflect that I've done the same for others before.

I was able to show them that stem-cell research is always going to be an issue for us because of the faith divisiveness, or where each of us stands on the scale. For example, are you in this extreme faith, evangelical camp or are you way over here at the Hindus' camp? Depending on where you are and the lens you look through, that is what really gives you your set of values on this issue. The audience was able to see that this was a template of how they can pursue these and other ethical questions with integrity.

I didn't give them answers. If they had asked me, I would have been happy to give them my personal perspective, but that wasn't my job. I felt that my job that day, and especially in ethics, was to get others to understand how our personal set of values influences our belief system and that no particular belief is the *right* one. So for me, that was the moment I recognized spirit at work. I remember on the drive back, just thanking God, "Thank you for allowing me to be a part of this, to be part of this dialogic interchange," and how graced I felt that this was something; it was important. I was making a contribution.

You can say, well, you didn't produce anything new — a serviceable product that people can wear or eat or drink. It wasn't like that; it was about *thoughts*. And to me, thoughts are things. It is a stage of a process that, depending on how much energy and collective thought have emerged together, allows us to create a new level of consciousness. So for me, that is a prime example of what we do here at this college, here in ethics.

We may never see the full results of it, meaning we might be here just to help plant some seeds. Finally, when other thoughts begin to collect into that one individual's mind and are recorded in whatever way, then perhaps it will manifest. There's the analogy of planting seeds: I feel like I do that a lot. To me, that is the most important work. If I ever experience the gift of actually seeing the harvest, I'd think, "Oh, that's heaven." That day at the teachers' convention, I not only planted seeds; I also saw the harvest.

NOREEN

An Educator Thrives on Transformation

It is in working with others that I find the excitement in transformation. Together we can find our new learning; together we can bounce ideas off each other. In my work, adults get to learn from kids and youths and seniors and look at things in a different way, and that is transforming. That is when I experience spirit at work.

In order for the spirit to have room to move and take flight, for me there needs to be a learning component. Let's take us somewhere we have never been before. That to me is the benefit of spirit at work. Let's go somewhere we haven't gone. Let's forge that new path somewhere else.

It is like singing in a choir. You cannot create the same effect singing alone as you can in a group. It is a completely different effect. An individual singing might still be very pleasant, but to hear a full choir with all the voices together — well, that is a different experience that takes you to a different place. It could not be reproduced by one person, but only works when you are all pulling together in the same direction. Take any team; sports has the same analogy. It is just because I work with music that this one comes to mind.

The advantage of creating sprit at work is that we are going somewhere we couldn't go to by ourselves and we will create something new. It might be something that we are not yet imagining, but maybe we will get there.

You have read the stories of others. We each have a story. What is yours?

chapter two

Getting a Grip on the Concept

How we experience spirit at work is highly subjective and transcendent, making it difficult to describe or define. Even though I can readily point out people who have spirit at work and can measure it, I find that spirit at work as a concept isn't that easy to explain. People who have had the experience themselves, even if it was only a fleeting moment, immediately have a sense of what it is. But those who struggle to find meaning in work often have no idea. I can now define spirit at work, but I still find that the best way to understand it is by helping a person get in touch with a time he or she had such an experience.

Each of us have had moments in our life when we knew we made the right career choice — moments when we felt really good about the work we were doing and what we were contributing to others. Think back over your work experience and recall a time when you felt most alive, most fulfilled or most excited about your work. A time when you really looked forward to going to work. This might be in your current position or in a job that you held previously. If a work experience does not come to mind, draw on another example when these feelings were alive, perhaps when you volunteered, were a member of a club or worked on a project or hobby. It does not matter whether you were paid.

If you are interested in your spirit-at-work score, completing the spirit-at-work assessment in the guidebook prior to doing the following reflection will give you a more accurate score.

Bring forth a time when you

- felt good about your work
- were engaged, excited and energized by work
- were committed to what you were doing
- felt like you were making a difference.

Can you remember what it felt like? What made it so exciting, engaging and energizing? What was your contribution? Think about the words you would use to describe that experience. Jot them down and be with them for a moment.

When I ask these questions in my workshops, I hear words like empowered, connected, valued, creative, purposeful, appreciated, validated, loving, responsible, authentic, achievement, contributing, teamwork, fun and encouraged. Are some of these words on your list?

The experience you recalled was likely a "peak experience" or what is often called a "mystical experience." You knew that you were making a difference. You knew that your work mattered. This is *spirit at work*.

· · · · · · ·

Spirit at work is about being fully engaged in our work. Feeling good about what we are doing and the contribution we are making. We tend to feel very connected to our colleagues and know that we share a common purpose. Spirit at work is also about being connected to something larger than self. And it often has a mystical component to it (a sense of perfection and transcendence). Let's look more closely at the four dimensions of spirit at work.

The Four Dimensions of Spirit at Work

I have had the joy of talking to many people who are passionate about their work. Although they all agreed they had spirit at work, they had a tendency to look at me with glazed eyes when I asked them to define it. Yet they found it very easy to recall and describe their experience. Although their stories were personal and individualized, the descriptions of their experiences of spirit at work were strikingly similar.

It became apparent through these conversations that spirit at work comprised four facets: engaging work, sense of community, spiritual connection and a mystical experience. As you read comments made by people with spirit at work, I invite you to think about your own experience of work. Which of these factors are present? Which areas could be cultivated?

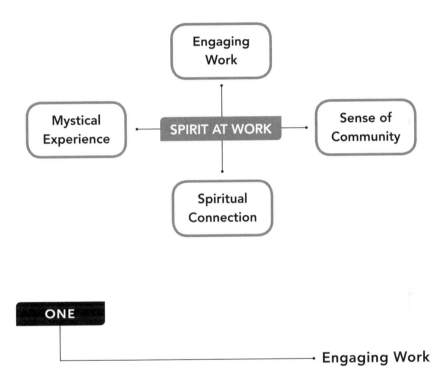

ONE

Engaging Work

Being engaged in our work involves seeing the higher purpose or meaning underlying our work; being authentic at work; having alignment between our values, beliefs and work; and feeling a sense of well-being.

Meaningful work. Perhaps the most important component of engaging work and spirit at work is that we feel we are making a difference; we are making a contribution towards others or a cause. Spirit at work involves having a higher purpose, being involved in meaningful and purposeful work, and serving others. It is through the act of service that we find meaning and purpose, at work or in other parts of our lives.

Listen how Donna, a physician, speaks about the meaning of her work:

> It felt warm, glorious and quivery inside. Like I had a reason to be on this earth. I had that sense that I had done something for this person and their loved ones. Yes. It worked. The treatment worked.

Many people believe that only certain jobs (such as those in the helping professions) are meaningful. But all work has a purpose. The work done by truck drivers, janitors, administrative support staff, factory workers, managers, sales clerks and plumbers is also purposeful. Many of us just haven't taken the time to get to the deeper meaning underlying these positions.

Similarly, all work is about service. It is easy to see how certain fields such as sales, the trades, hairdressing and medicine are about serving the customer, client or patient. If we go deeper, though, we will discover that every job is serving someone or a cause.

Many people are doing meaningful and important work, but they do not experience spirit at work. It is important that people are not only engaged in meaningful work, but *feel* that what they are doing is meaningful. That is the key. Kelly, a nurse turned organizational consultant, knows that.

> The individual has to see the meaning and purpose in it for the spirit part to work. Lots of people don't link their work to the greater good or highest good for all. I went into my role very much believing that I was a public servant. I'm doing this because I believe in the work I am doing. It is meaningful work and it is going to make a contribution.

I am often asked if someone who is doing bad things (e.g., a member of a gang or terrorist group) could have spirit at work. I would argue that although it may look like the elements of spirit at work are present, what is missing is the contribution for the higher good, and the fact that no one gets hurt in the process. When people experience spirit at work, they and others need to view the contribution as for the greater good of *all* — as something larger than each of the individuals doing the work. The ultimate purpose is making sure that the intent is for a higher good.

Authenticity. Authenticity is about being who we are all the time, even at work. It means speaking and living with honesty and integrity. To be authentic, our actions must be congruent with our inner values and beliefs. Often referred to as "bringing your whole person to work," authenticity involves integrating our physical, mental, emotional and spiritual energies at work. This bringing together of the body, mind, heart and spirit promotes wholeness rather than the fragmentation of self so often experienced in the workplace.

So, if we are looking to be authentic at work, comments like "Leave your ego at the door" or "There is no room for emotions here" or "Intuition has no role in the workplace" no longer fit. Kelly, the nurse turned organizational consultant, spoke about what it was like to be authentic:

> I'm the same person all the time. I'm not one person at work, another person at home and another person while I'm playing. I'm the same person, so I don't have a work face, which a lot of people do.

Authenticity is about the extent to which we feel we can *express our complete selves* at work. Expressing our complete selves at work allows us to be all of who we are. It facilitates passion and creative expression, making it much easier to live in alignment.

Alignment. When we are aligned, there is harmony between our inner selves and our work. We experience congruity between our values and beliefs and the work we do, the people we work with and ultimately the organization we work for. The more aligned our work is with our higher purpose, the deeper our experience of spirit at work.

Betty, a business partner, uses the analogy of a tuning fork to describe the sense of alignment she had with her colleagues:

> I understand tuning forks. If it's in tune, then when you hit the note that's in tune, the tuning fork starts to sing. The frequencies are close enough together that they are in harmony, so one makes the other one start to resonate. As I think about who's around me now, there is a compatibility or a "something" where it's harmonious and synergistic.

When everything is in alignment, work is said to "flow," to be easy and joyful. We experience a sense of well-being.

Sense of well-being. When we have spirit at work, we often have profound feelings of joy and well-being. We are excited by the assignments and challenges that come our way. We have fun at work. As Kelly, the nurse turned organizational consultant, said, "It's almost past describing because it felt so good."

So many people I spoke to talked about feelings of love, of work being joyful and peaceful, and of being grateful for the work they do. Here's how Frank, a regional coordinator for the handicapped, described his work: "There's a real sense of joy about it, a real sense of excitement and a sense of gratitude to be part of something that's so significant and so important."

They portray their work as fulfilling their personal mission or calling. A consultant and facilitator, Don makes this typical declaration: "This is my life's work. I cannot *not* be doing this. It has found me as much as I have found it."

Others, like the physician Donna, say there is no other work they would prefer.

> It is a privilege to be a part of helping. Privilege is an important word because my patients don't have to come to me. It is a privilege that they trust me enough to let me treat them — like that is a sacred trust here.

TWO

Sense of Community

The second dimension of spirit at work is a sense of community, best described as feeling connected to others at work and through work. This sense of connection involves feelings of trust, mutual respect and a shared purpose with our co-workers.

Sense of connection. A sense of connection refers to the extent to which we feel like we belong at work. We are a part of a community, part of a team where others care about us and we care about them. We know that we matter. Everyone knows that our work is important and that we need to work together to achieve common goals. When this connection permeates the workplace, it doesn't matter if you are the

CEO, janitor, receptionist or someone in between; everyone shares the connection. Jason recalls:

> I will never forget the first time I participated in a "code." I don't think any nurse ever forgets that. I was working in emergency that evening and a young girl came in with what seemed to be an asthma attack. She was extremely short of breath. No sooner had she walked into emergency than she went into respiratory arrest. She just stopped breathing and collapsed, unconscious. Everyone immediately stopped what they were doing and focused on bringing this girl back. A couple of nurses picked her up and ran with her into a room. Someone else got her on oxygen. The doctor gave her medications while someone else set up an intravenous tube. A lab technician started drawing blood. All the time, someone else was trying to locate her next of kin. It really felt like everyone was an essential part of the team. We didn't know if we were going to be able to keep her alive, and whether she would suffer brain damage if we did. It didn't matter. In that moment, we were united in our efforts. We truly felt like we were part of a team. We were connected and I suspect will always feel connected to one another.

Trust, respect and love. This sense of connection also involves trust and respect among the people with whom you are working. It sometimes includes feelings of love — not romantic love, but more like a deep, heartfelt love shared by good friends.

When a sense of personal connection and trust exists we are able to be authentic and say things that are important, knowing that we will feel heard and respected by others. Frank, regional coordinator for the handicapped, describes his experience with his colleagues, which illustrates the point beautifully:

> None of us as individuals were in a position to do all the tasks we did, by ourselves. It became pretty apparent that we all needed to work together to achieve the goals we all shared, so we developed a sense of community and common purpose that was inspiring, I think, for all of us. It feels to me that at some level we all shared a love with each other and for each other and for the common purpose. And love isn't too strong a word. There was a real sense of personal connection and trust. We could say things that were really important to us,

knowing that we would be heard and respected by others and our advice would be acted upon and affirmed.

Shared purpose. Sharing a sense of purpose and meaning with our co-workers about our work contributes to our feelings of community at work and our spirit at work. Connection with others, along with a common purpose, goes a long way to achieving mutual goals.

Those who experience spirit at work recognize that they are part of something larger than the sum of the individuals with whom they are involved, and that they need each other to be successful, as was the case in the emergency situation described above. Through this connection, people often experience success previously unavailable to them as an individual or organization. These moments of deep connection with others can be so strong that people feel them even when working alone. This occurs especially when we are deeply committed to a cause. Jim, a writer, described what it was like for him:

> I've felt like I was accompanied by lots of people — like I was only one of many people who shared this idea or dream or experience, although I was actually acting alone at the time.

THREE

→ **Spiritual Connection**

The meaning of spirituality. Before I get into the details of this dimension, I would like to talk about terminology. It is so easy to get hung up on words and their connotation and miss the essence of the meaning. The terms "spirit, spiritual and spirituality" are often used interchangeably. Although there are various schools of thought on spirituality — including religious, metaphysical and humanistic[1] — the common essence is that spirituality encompasses "a search for meaning, for unity, for connectedness to nature, humanity and the transcendent."[2] Rather than adopting any particular school of thought, this illuminates the common essence of all — a search for meaning and connectedness.

Other definitions of spirit and spirituality that fit with this universal understanding are:

- ⤸ "the basic feeling of being connected with one's complete self, others and the entire universe" in a common purpose[3]
- ⤸ "an animating life force, an energy that inspires one toward certain ends or purposes that go beyond self,"[4] and
- ⤸ "a continuing search for meaning and purpose in life; an appreciation for the depth of life; the expanse of the universe and natural forces which operate; a personal belief system."[5]

It seems that the search for meaning is ever-increasing, and nowhere is the search growing faster than in the workplace. Why? Many of us are demoralized, stressed and experiencing spiritual disorientation as a result of the downsizing, reengineering and cutbacks within our organizations. Our relationship with our work and employer has changed. We may have lost our way. We are questioning the relationship between spirituality and our work and are seeking work that is inspiring and meaningful. It is no longer enough to collect a salary from our employer. We are looking for a spiritual connection.

People who experience spirit at work have what I call a spiritual connection. They are aware of the influence of their spirituality or deeply held values on their work experience. Many are also aware of a sense of love that they hold for others through their work.

Connection to something larger than self. Most people who experience spirit at work sense we are all connected and not alone. They are aware of the connection to a higher power, nature, humanity or the universe. The examples that follow will give you an idea of the breadth of this notion of a spiritual connection.

People like Kelly (the nurse turned organizational consultant) and Donna (the physician) feel that spirit comes through them from another source. Says Kelly:

> We just basically see ourselves as portals almost for the universe to work through, because I know it is not me. I just happen to be the vehicle.

Many, like Frank, the regional coordinator for the handicapped, spoke of being guided. "It seemed like we received some inspiration, like there was something happening in the room that was guided in some way."

For some, this presence or guidance was, or came from, God or a Supreme Being: "A truly emotional moment where I felt God was present, like I wasn't alone — unseen hands were guiding me," said Harry, a lieutenant colonel.

Others referred to this spiritual connection as "God within," "God-like" and spoke of a Creator or Universal Source. One said:

> There is the capital "S" Spirit working through us, in us, about us. You can use God or Creator or the Universal Source or whatever your language; that spirit is always at work.

As Jim, a writer, put it:

> I immediately discovered Spirit — a true relationship with the Divine — not the religious ideal but the personal experience of being connected with some force that we might call God or Goddess or Nature or All That Is.

Finally, here's how Phil, a chairman, distinguished between work and spirituality: "I don't believe in spirit as a theological or supernatural entity. I define it in psychological terms — the whole of emotions, energy and vitality, body and values."

These examples show that there are several ways to experience a spiritual connection at work. The key is the awareness of a connection with something larger than self.

Positive effect on work. Although this presence was experienced in different ways, the outcome was amazingly similar. This connection with *a greater source* always seemed to have a positive effect on the person's work. For some, the awareness of this spiritual presence was enough to feel a sense of comfort in making difficult decisions, knowing that they were not alone. Others were aware of how the inspiration or guidance helped them make better choices. Yet others spoke of the direct help they received when they surrendered and asked for assistance when they ran out of ideas or the situation appeared hopeless.

Kevin, an emergency room doctor, sought me out after he heard me speak about spirit at work and the influence of a spiritual connection on our work. Let me tell you about the story he shared for the first time.

Kevin was on shift at the emergency department of a large urban hospital. As usual, the waiting room was full, the wait was long and people were getting testy. Yet he liked the energy and camaraderie that came with working in emergency. He liked how he was able to make an immediate difference in the lives of his patients. As he moved from patient to patient, he was aware of being tired, but also of feeling good about his competence and how he was present with each patient — until he was assigned to Sylvia.

Sylvia was forty-eight years old and very sick. Her temperature was off the scale. She complained of a persistent headache and a stiff and painful neck. She was showing signs of confusion and it was becoming nearly impossible to communicate with her. Having ruled out all other potential diagnoses, Kevin's mind turned to the possibility of bacterial meningitis. If his hunch were true, Kevin knew that time was not on his side. On his orders, nursing staff quickly prepared a room and prepped Sylvia for a spinal tap — a procedure whereby spinal fluid is removed from the patient's spine. It's a relatively simple procedure, although most patients end up with a severe headache.

Kevin became aware of his discomfort as he entered the room and began to put on gloves. He no longer had an air of competence. He knew that Sylvia was obese, but it now hit him how obese she was. How was he ever going to direct the needle through her body in order to puncture her spine and remove the spinal fluid? He could feel the tension in the room. Everyone knew it was an impossible feat. And yet what were his choices? He was the doctor.

As he took the needle in his hand, he said a prayer and asked for guidance. He knew he could not do this alone. He needed to surrender, and surrender he did. He watched as the needle effortlessly glided through Sylvia's body and he was able to withdraw some spinal fluid. It was if he were an instrument, a conduit, holding the needle as some Higher Power did his work. He knew it wasn't him. The look on a nurse's face and in her eyes told him that she knew it wasn't, either. They had just been part of a Divine intervention. Kevin quietly looked up and expressed thanks.

Love for others. As our experience of spirit at work deepens, many of us become aware of a sense of love we have for humankind. This is different than the love that's part of a sense of community. When we feel we are part of a community, we often feel loved, but when we are aware of a spiritual connection, we often feel love towards others. This love tends to be expressed through compassion, kindness, service and going the extra mile.

Given our desire for more meaning and enlightenment in our lives, I am not surprised that people with spirit at work have this awareness and feel its positive impact on their work. In another research project, I looked at the personality of people with spirit at work and found that they have what I would call an "integrated personality." More than the five personality factors[6] (extraversion, emotional stability, conscientiousness, agreeableness and openness to experiences), they also seem to be spiritually inclined. This discovery fits well with a recent proposition that spirituality is a sixth personality factor.[7] I find this very exciting, as the research suggests that personality is fully developed by around age thirty, whereas our spirituality grows throughout our whole life. Perhaps this is why spirit at work can be cultivated at any stage of life.

FOUR

Mystical Experience

Most people describe their spirit-at-work experience as including a mystical dimension. Earlier in this chapter, you identified a time you felt alive, engaged and excited at work. That was most likely a mystical experience. We have all had them. Think of watching a sunset with a loved one, the birth of a child or a time you were totally enthralled at a music concert. Those were mystical moments. I am sure that you can recall others. We are just not used to thinking about them in a work environment. Kevin's experience of Divine intervention was most likely a mystical experience.

Mystical encounters at work include moments when we are in a state of positive arousal or energy. These are the times we experience a sense of perfection, awe, complete joy and bliss. Note that people who enjoy spirit at work are not in a continuous mystical state. However, the more they experience spirit at work, the more they enjoy these blissful times.

State of positive arousal or energy. Many people spoke about a physical sensation, describing it as a peak experience, a natural high, fun, total bliss, being in the zone. Phil, the chairman, described spirit at work as "a burst of excitement in my body."

"It was like being in the zone," Harry, the lieutenant colonel, said, "putting out 110 percent, seeming to know the what, why, how, where, when, who in order to tackle whatever problem hit the fan."

"The experiences were just extraordinary," Frank, the regional coordinator for the handicapped, added. "It felt like it wasn't a job; it wasn't work. I was doing something really important, and as a bonus, I was getting paid for it."

Sense of perfection. Most people with mystical experiences at work say their work is characterized by a sense of perfection and effortless energy. As Bill, a management professor, put it:

> It was total bliss, as if everything was perfect, which it was. I was feeling as if I was "in the moment," not being hurried by tasks, deadlines or activities, but by a connection with a greater source that had a wonderful effect on the workplace at that moment. It was genuine, authentic, and everything seemed to make sense. I actually felt like I saw a much bigger picture of work and how all the various aspects fit into one.

For many, the experiences of spirit at work were also awe-inspiring, mysterious or sacred, and had a transcendent nature to them. "I was in 'a flow state' so that I felt pulled along in something over which I had only partial control," said Jim, the writer.

Complete joy and bliss. Joy, bliss or ecstasy at work — a feeling of energy or vitality often difficult to describe — is a common and recurring experience to those who have spirit at work. Kelly, the nurse turned organizational consultant, described her experience at work as a natural high. "You almost don't come down for a while afterward, because it feels so good."

People who experience spirit at work often lose their sense of time. They may be so engaged that five hours passes but it feels like twenty minutes. They are so present and living in the moment that they are unaware of their surroundings. Myron, a chaplain and business professor, describes a blissful time he had teaching a university class:

> I was totally present to the class and the topic. It was not an "aha" experience, but the culmination of a series of successful interactions with the students. It just seemed to flow and I did not feel forced or out of my depth.

Spirit at work is a distinct and very identifiable state. Even if we haven't had the experience ourselves, we are quick to identify others who have. It is that obvious.

A Definition of Spirit at Work

So what is spirit at work? Spirit at work is comprised of four elements: engaging work, sense of community, spiritual connection and mystical experience.

Engaging work involves the belief that work is meaningful and has a higher purpose. Our values and beliefs are aligned with our work. We are authentic and experience a profound sense of well-being at work.

A *sense of community* arises from sharing a common purpose with others and being connected through feelings of trust, respect and love.

A *spiritual connection* is about being connected to something larger than self that has a positive effect on the workplace. It often involves a sense of love for others.

Mystical experiences are those times in which we feel vital, energized, and have a sense of joy and bliss at work.

1. Are you fully engaged in your work?

2. What do you need to do to be authentic at work?

3. Is the work you do in alignment with your beliefs and values?

4. What is the deeper meaning that underlies your work?

5. What does it mean to have a sense of community at your workplace? What might it look like?

6. How would you describe your spiritual connection at work?

7. Can you recall a time that your spirituality or deeply held values influenced how you were at work?

8. Have you ever had a mystical experience at work? If so, what was it that made that experience mystical? If not, visualize what it would be like to have a mystical experience at work.

chapter three

Defining Moments as a Window to Spirit at Work

Most people who enjoy spirit at work recall defining moments, that is, significant events or experiences that influenced their world view, career choice or both. These individuals suggest that it was those defining moments that put them onto the path of spirit at work, or at least helped them make decisions that would influence them in that direction.

Defining moments range from parents teaching them as children to listen to their voice, to a moment of enlightenment regarding career choice, to changing jobs. Some cite the influence of a movie's message or an actual experience of spirit at work or a response to a difficult childhood. Many people can identify the exact moment and circumstances associated with choosing their career or gaining clarity about their world view, because it was a very significant event in their lives. It was a defining moment.

When I asked Sandra about how she came to be a police officer, she responded:

> It is very simple. I never knew that I was interested in policing at all. I wanted to be a lawyer. That was the only thing I aspired to be — for no particular reason. Then my dad heard that the RCMP had a summer program that paid students to learn about policing. He suggested I attend to learn about aspects of law that law school wouldn't teach me. I agreed. So I applied and got the position and started working that summer. I was a special constable. I got a uniform and I got all the equipment

except the gun. I was always with another constable — basically my trainer — and I just went around with him, like his partner. He took the lead in everything, and I was just there to help him and take statements. I learned a lot of stuff. In the end, I did pretty much everything they did. I just learned as I went along. By the second summer, I was driving around by myself, writing tickets and stuff, and I really got a good feeling for the job.

It took me about a month to know what I wanted to do. I was driving along with Mike, a sergeant at the time. I just turned to him and I said, "Mike, I've fallen in love with this job. I love this job."

And he goes, "Yeah, I kind of noticed that."

And I said, "I can't think of anything else. This is what I want to do for the rest of my life."

It probably was not as big a moment for him. He said, "Oh yeah, that's nice."

And I said, "Okay, I think I am going to write the test and try to get in." From that moment, I knew that police work was what I wanted to do, and I haven't changed my mind since.

Whereas Sandra's defining moment occurred when she was a young adult participating in a summer program, Larry's defining moment happened when he was twelve years old. His ongoing contact with his dentist inspired him to pursue a career in dentistry.

I had some major surgery on my gums and bone after an accident. I enjoyed the people who did the work on me. My dentist was into it, just totally immersed in his work — friendly, happy, never miserable. I think I have tried to emulate him in my practice. He was considered one of the top dentists in North America. He graduated extremely high in his class. The fact that I became a dentist while he was still a dentist made me a contemporary of his, and that was really a high point of my life, an emotional thing. I was honored when chosen to give him his fortieth-year award, but I knew I was going to be emotional. My wife said, "You shouldn't even give the award because you are going to cry." I did give it to him and I did cry. I am not ashamed of it at all. I would cry again, because he meant the world to me as a kid. He is the one who inspired me to be a dentist. I loved the way he served as a dentist and I wanted to be like him.

Karla knew that she was ready for a career change, but to what?

> I had reached a point in my career where I knew I wanted to do something different. I didn't know what, but I had decided to leave my work in a year. I put the money together, put the plan into place and got really focused. Six months into that year, I still wasn't sure what I was going to do. Then I came across an ad in the paper describing the landscape architecture technologist program at a local technical school. And that was just it.
>
> I hadn't known the program existed. I was on a business flight one morning, reading the newspaper. The sun was coming through the window and it shone on the ad like a spotlight. "That is interesting," I thought. I put the paper down but couldn't leave it there. I pulled it up again. That moment had such clarity around it. It was such a — boom — "You have to call this number. You have to find out about this."

In response to growing up in an unhappy and dysfunctional family, Donna the physician made a conscious decision to live her life differently. Her defining moment was the promise she made to herself while in her late teens:

> I will not live my life this way. I will live each day in such a way that if I die at the end of the day, I'll be able to say, "That's okay. It was a good day." That was a defining moment. I mean, a lot of things fell into place at that point. I wonder if I would have made the choices I have made otherwise?

While that moment influenced how Donna would live her life, she experienced another defining moment in midlife that influenced how she did her work. As she observed her father's anger with his own death, she concluded that there was another way to deal with one's demise. As a physician, she found ways to ease terminally ill patients into death that became an important and fulfilling part of her work.

• • • • • • •

Most people I interviewed for this book mentioned a relationship between defining moments and spirit at work. Defining moments influenced whether they experienced spirit at work, the path they took to spirit at work, the intensity of their spirit at work and the decision to make meaningful career choices.

Defining Moments: Assessing the Impact on Your Work

We have all had defining moments in our lives — experiences that influenced who we are, what we value and what directions we took in our lives. What about you? How have defining moments influenced your spirit at work?

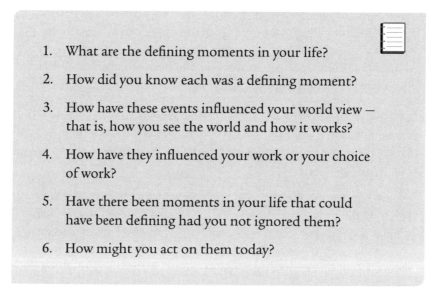

1. What are the defining moments in your life?

2. How did you know each was a defining moment?

3. How have these events influenced your world view — that is, how you see the world and how it works?

4. How have they influenced your work or your choice of work?

5. Have there been moments in your life that could have been defining had you not ignored them?

6. How might you act on them today?

chapter four

Which Path Are You On?

How did these people get to have spirit at work? Why do they have spirit at work and others don't? Although we tend to experience spirit at work in a similar way, we get there in different ways.

Some people have always had spirit at work. If you are one of them, you are probably reading this book to see how you can achieve even deeper spirit at work. If so, you will not be disappointed. For others, spirit at work develops over time, and at some point — often at midlife — it comes together. For a third group, spirit at work occurs as a response to a crisis or personal event — a response that, for many, becomes transformative.

Finally, there is a group of people who, shall we say, wear their spirit at work on their sleeves. Their experience of spirit at work is in direct relationship with their experience at work. If things are going well at work, they have spirit at work. If things are not going so well, they don't have spirit at work.

I call these the four paths to spirit at work. I now want to introduce you to Larry, Noreen, Ben and Sheila, and briefly discuss the paths they took. Larry's path was *always there*. Noreen took the *coming together* path. Ben experienced the path of *transformative events* and Sheila is on the *contextual sensitivity* path.

Always there. Larry has been a dentist for more than thirty years. He has always had spirit at work, has always loved his work. He describes himself as a people person who helps out, cares for others, and is simply dedicated to what he does. That was how he grew up; that is what his family did. For him, the experience of spirit at work was constant, with peaks but never valleys along the way. When I asked how he developed spirit at work, he credited "gifts I have been given."

"It's in me," he added. Unlike people who believe everyone is born with spirit and each of us chooses whether to develop it or not, Larry believes we either have it or don't. "You have to come into the world at least half-cocked," he joked.

Coming together. Noreen, an educator, feels that while it is possible to experience fleeting moments of spirit at work as a young adult, she is more typical in coming across it later in life. Only in midlife had she acquired enough diverse experiences in life to make the connections. She describes her skills, faith and passion coming together such that she suddenly felt "at home." All previous roles — as a mother, wife and teacher — worked to prepare her for the experience. Noreen believes that, "Spirit at work is related to midlife, a time when you are pulling everything together."

Transformative events. Ben is a physiotherapist whose work has changed over time. The more experienced he became, the more his skill level increased, resulting in constant improvement. His transformation occurred when he took an acupuncture course where he learned about holistic medicine. This precipitated the biggest change in his life, both personally and professionally. He says that, "It was life-transforming. It changed everything." Transformative events can relate to spiritual growth or a personal crisis. Later in this chapter, I will talk about the path of transformative events as a result of a personal crisis.

Contextual sensitivity. Sheila loves her work as a graduate coordinator and administrative assistant but experiences spirit at work only when her work setting allows it. For her, it's up to how the leaders run the organization, how well they promote teamwork, and how they recognize and treat each employee. When her boss is supportive and inclusive, she has spirit at work. But when the organization casts a negative influence, she has seen herself change from a committed to a bitter employee. She was only able to regain her spirit at work by moving to a new organization. Sheila is on the contextually sensitive path to spirit at work, one that is dependent on the work environment.

These brief profiles illustrate the four distinct paths to spirit at work. Most people have to work at cultivating their spirit at work, and for this they must be internally motivated. Even individuals on the *always there* path find that the reflection and exercises in this book help them achieve a fuller spirit-at-work experience.

Let's look at these paths a little more closely. As you read the stories, see if you can identify your path.

The Four Paths to Spirit at Work

ONE

The Path of Always There

Some people with spirit at work told me they have always experienced work in this way. Ken, the parking attendant, said, "I don't know if you develop it. I think you have it or you don't." Yet each person on the always-there path spoke about having strong influences in their lives and what I call "defining moments" in their early years. So were they born with a predisposition to spirit at work or were they were influenced in their early years to eventually enjoy spirit at work?

Kelly, the nurse turned organizational consultant, says that everyone is born with spirit and therefore has the capacity for spirit at work. She believes that it is a matter of whether we develop it or use it. This book is based on the belief that we all have the capacity for spirit at work and that it is inside each of us, waiting to be developed.

People who experience spirit at work as *always there* speak about being outgoing and regularly helping others out. For example, Larry, the dentist, recalls helping others at a young age.

> I have always been a people person. I was always into helping people, and I never realized until fairly recently that it's partly because I grew up with both sets of grandparents, who lived in

my hometown. I always cared for them, was visiting them, driving them places, doing things for them. We lived on a street leading to the seniors' lodge, so we often found ourselves helping an old person who had just stumbled or was carrying groceries and had fallen.

We just did that without thinking about it. Actually, my whole family was really involved with people. We cared about people. We did things for people on request and just because we wanted to.

For this group of individuals, spirit at work was constant, cutting across a range of jobs. For example, such people included a receptionist, organizational consultant, dentist and parking attendant. Molly, currently a receptionist and bookkeeper, said, "I think no matter where I worked, I loved it." Prior to becoming a receptionist, Molly worked as a nursing assistant in a hospital. She also worked in a lounge and restaurant, serving tables, washing floors and scrubbing bathrooms. "I did the whole works. It didn't matter what it was — I did it and I thoroughly enjoyed it," she said.

Similarly, Ken, the parking lot attendant, could not remember a time when spirit at work was not present for him. For Kelly, "It has been a constant. I have always felt connected."

Although the experience is constant for some people, they describe the intensity of the experience as varying over time. For example, Kelly noticed a gradual increase in her consciousness of the connection and has felt it grow deeper.

On the other hand, Larry describes his experience as more even.

My love and desire for work hasn't waned in thirty-one years. I have never, never in thirty years woken up and said, "Oh God, it is Monday morning." It is more like I snap my fingers on Monday morning and say, "Here we go! We've got another week ahead of us!" And I don't know what does it. I really don't know what does it, but it's in me. That is all I can say. I am glad to be alive. I am glad to go to work. I am glad to be doing what I am doing.

How many of us can say that about our work? Can you imagine what it would be like not to dread Mondays, to look forward to another week? And we can.

TWO

The Path of Coming Together

Most of us experience spirit at work as a "coming together." Unlike people for whom spirit at work is a constant, people in the *coming together* group believe that spirit at work is something that develops over time, something constantly worked on. People in this *coming together* group experience spirit at work only when their abilities, experience and passion come together. Some say it is a point of "feeling at home" or "having arrived," when they are aware of a match between their passion, gifts and work, and believe that a transformation has occurred.

Noreen is a former elementary school teacher, now a church educator. Although she was passionate about teaching, she found it draining. Noreen recalls fleeting moments when she got a taste of spirit at work but wasn't able to sustain it in her teaching role. She felt herself breaking down and opted to leave the profession. Today she's still working as an educator but in a different environment — and she regularly experiences spirit at work. Noreen is fully engaged in her work, shares a sense of community and common purpose with her colleagues, and continues to have a spirit connection. This is how she speaks about her work today:

> I am in a rare position where my teaching skills, faith and passion have come together in this position. I feel more at home than I have felt in a long time. My roles as teacher, mom and wife prepared me for what I am doing now. All of these parts coming together add up to a transformation.

For some people, this "coming together" was less than smooth. Maureen the hairdresser describes her life as a roller coaster ride. She moved back and forth between careers in music and hairdressing, she was in and out of relationships, she moved back to her country of origin and then, when she came back to Canada, she worked for two hair salons that went bankrupt. In reflecting on her story, Maureen suggests:

> I was trying on all of these hats. I always knew that I loved styling hair and music, but other stuff — friends, activities — kind of got

in the way. I don't think I knew myself. I didn't know what I was about, which direction I needed to go in. A lot of it is youth. You kind of do what your friends do. I wasn't happy with who I was, working in the wrong places. I had to work my way out of that self-discovery process before I could get to that place.

For those in the *coming together* group, the experience of spirit at work is incremental, something that developed over time. As the physician Donna explains, "It gets better with time. It gets richer with every significant event and with age."

Here's Karla, the landscape designer:

Things have built on each other, and although I have left certain experiences behind, I have also been very aware of pulling a lot forward with me. Part of that is age and the building of experiences. Now I can play in the arena that draws on all of my life experiences.

Spirit at work as a midlife phenomenon. For many people in the *coming together* group, spirit at work has been a midlife occurrence. Midlife is typically a time when we re-examine our values and beliefs. We start to think about the legacy we want to leave. We get in touch with our mortality. We question whether our life and work is having any impact. But why do we need to wait until our life is half over before we do that? People who explore these deeper questions earlier in life tend to enjoy spirit at work at a much younger age.

Rowena, a university professor, says she led a spiritual life and her faith significantly influenced how she lived and worked. Even so, it was not until midlife that she experienced spirit at work. Now that she is older, she finds she asks different questions.

I am more interested in what legacy we are going to leave for those coming after us. At the end of my life, if I can feel that I helped in some marginal way to increase the common good, I will feel like I have participated in the will of God and the will of good and the will of spirit.

Rowena started asking questions about her potential legacy when she first saw spirit at work and recognized the huge difference it made in work outcomes. She regards spirit at work as a midlife experience, a time of putting everything together. So does Maureen the hairdresser:

> I feel really complete. I was a late bloomer, I guess, but now I have come to a place where I know how I want to do things. It's like my life began at a very late age. I finally feel like a grown-up. I am happy with who I am now.

As she and her medical practice age, Donna finds that she is more reflective, which has resulted in increasingly rich experiences. Spiritual growth was the precipitating factor.

Even though spirit at work can take time to emerge, everyone on this path eventually got a taste of it. Noreen talks about the fleeting moments that kept her going, and Maureen recalls the times when everything went well and she clicked with clients who kept her in the field for twenty-six years. What fostered spirit at work for Noreen, Maureen and others was a coming together of their passion, values, abilities and experiences, combined with reflexivity, self-discovery and engagement in activities they felt were important.

• • • • • • •

Spirit at work is a journey. And along that journey, Karla said, "Know that you need to release, modify or change some things, and keep others. Just by reshaping some things, you'll see that you can use them."

I became aware of spirit at work as a journey when I asked people to rate themselves on a spirit-at-work scale. When I asked them to rate their spirit at work from zero to ten, they seemed hesitant to rate themselves too high because, as one person suggested, "I still see a larger coming together in the future." For example, the physician Donna assigned herself a rating of seven to eight out of ten because, she said, "I just don't know what is out there. I know where I have been, but I am assuming there is a lot more."

So if we are on the *coming together* path, spirit at work will be incremental; it will develop over time. We will have the sense that we have arrived when our life experiences, skills and passions come together and we live in alignment with what matters. At that point, we will feel whole and integrated as opposed to broken and segmented, as so many of us feel today.

THREE

The Path of Transformative Events

The third path to spirit at work comes as a result of a "transformative event." Stuff happens. We get sick. We are diagnosed with a debilitating disease, maybe one that is terminal. Our marriage ends in divorce. Our children make bad choices with negative and long-lasting results. The company we work for downsizes or goes under or our spouse loses his or her job. We lose a loved one. The path of *transformative events* occurs in response to a crisis or spiritual awakening.

Rose began a career in real estate when she was in her late thirties. At that point she would have rated her experience of spirit at work a two or three out of ten because she was using work as an excuse to get away from social obligations. She enjoyed her work, but not as she currently does.

The turning point for Rose was when her husband died and she discovered she was ineligible for benefits. Her husband always joked that he was worth more dead than alive, but when the time came, a glitch in paperwork and procedures proved that to be untrue. Rose was left on her own to raise a family.

> It was absolutely devastating. That is when I started working much harder than normal. When Mike died, I wanted to give the boys a good life and send them to university. I really got into it and it became my whole life. The more I worked, the more I liked it.

Rose invested herself in her work because she had to earn a living in order to raise her family, not because it was her passion. Initially, meaning came from providing for her children, but in time she came to love it. Now, she says she loves everything about it and views her work as a "very good service I can give to people."

Rose currently gives herself a ten out of ten in terms of her spirit at work and refers to real estate as what makes her tick, the central part of her life. Even now, well into her eighties, Rose cannot envision a time she will not be selling real estate. Had she not been widowed, she believes her life would have turned out differently, that she would probably have put her energy into social events rather than work.

Whereas a personal crisis forged Rose's transformative path, Ben described a spiritual awakening as the origin of his transformation. Ben is a physiotherapist whose mother was also a physiotherapist, so he was exposed to the profession early. More importantly, his awareness of how much his mother cared is what drew him to the profession. He liked the idea of being hands-on and interacting with the client.

But his path changed once he took an acupressure course, which he said helped him form an entire philosophy for how to go about his practice. He refers to the class as transforming his life in terms of relationships and everyday conversations as well as career. The class's influence was so great that Ben even questions whether he would have remained in physiotherapy without it. "I would call it a transition point. A big change in how I looked at people. It changed everything."

Ben says that before taking the course, he was focusing only on the physical aspect at work and missing the bigger picture. He was not integrating the whole person. Attending the course helped him to see the value of including every aspect of that person's life, including emotional, mental and spiritual, which he says now gets carried into every conversation or relationship.

Like individuals on the coming together path, Rose the real estate agent and Ben the physiotherapist had moments that inspired them to remain in their careers. However, it was only when they experienced a significant event that they found spirit at work. Clearly, *transformative events* — including a spiritual awakening, epiphany or significant life event — can precipitate spirit at work.

On the other hand, a personal crisis (as Rose experienced) seems to demand a response before it results in spirit at work. The response then turns a difficult event into a transformative event. Individuals often begin to question their values, life priorities and lifestyle, a process sure to affect their relationship with work.

In this way, significant life events — including job loss, organizational takeovers, downsizing, serious accidents, divorce or the loss of a loved one — become opportunities as well as challenges. Once the necessary grieving has taken place, times of crisis offer the potential for growth and change.

FOUR

The Path of Contextual Sensitivity

Aspects of where we work, including the leadership, the culture and our relationship with our colleagues, definitely impacts how we feel about work. But for some of us, the organizational environment ultimately determines whether we experience spirit at work. I call this the path of *contextual sensitivity*.

The path of contextual sensitivity is clearly different from the paths previously outlined. Because it is influenced greatly by the work environment, spirit at work comes and goes. When it goes, people who have previously experienced it often work very hard to get it back, even if that means changing employment.

Sheila works as a graduate coordinator and administrative assistant. Even though she gives herself a ten out of ten in terms of her spirit at work, she experienced two periods where she lost her spirit at work and had to change jobs to regain it. For her, the difference between having and not having spirit at work involved leadership and a sense of team.

Because of the influence of the organization, Sheila changed from a caring and committed employee to one who was bitter and indifferent. She felt disrespected, degraded, blocked and put down, felt that her services were not needed, felt she was given no information and had no sense of belonging. She became bitter and adopted the attitude, "I'm going on a coffee break and I don't care if he calls" or "I'll just sleep in and be late."

Unhappy with who she had become, Sheila eventually changed jobs. In the new workplace, she immediately felt included, challenged, supported, respected, trusted, valued, involved in rewarding work and recognized for her contribution. After three years in the new position, Sheila continues to experience high levels of spirit at work. She feels highly motivated and involved; she finds it rewarding. "They do not view me as a secretary or receptionist. They actually see me as being an expert in my field. So I'm committed to doing well no matter what the problem is."

The person was the same. The organizational features were different. The outcomes were opposite.

Sandra, the police officer introduced in Chapter One, also gave herself a ten out of ten in terms of her spirit at work, until she had a work-related brush with death. After somebody tried to kill her, that changed everything, including her rating. Even though she still experiences "tens" regularly, now she ranks her average as eight.

> In the beginning, I was gung-ho and ready to go — which I still am. I never changed my ethic or how happy I am to be at work, but obviously I had a real bad experience. The scare factor made me feel I couldn't do the job anymore. I really went down and sort of stayed ho-hum for a couple of months.

Out of fear, she was focusing on her own safety. She kept her head low, avoiding stressful situations and putting in minimal effort.

Once Sandra became aware of how strongly the fear had settled in, and how it impacted the way she worked, she knew that she had to do something about it. Her passion was still to help others and work on the police force, but she realized that her fear was compromising that. So she got special counseling to overcome her fear and regain her spirit at work.

Like Sandra, Sheila, the administrative assistant, felt a sense of responsibility and commitment to make the team work. She was committed to and loved her work, but that was not enough to keep her on the *always there* path.

> If you're well-suited to the job and you're allowed to flourish, you have a very happy environment. If your personality is stifled, you will be a very unhappy person and won't last.

The path of *contextual sensitivity* demonstrates that the work environment influences spirit at work. While organizational factors play a part in all the various paths to spirit at work, the effect is much stronger for those on the contextually sensitive path. Their spirit depends on leadership, inclusion, respect, support, teamwork and recognition.

Just as important, those who lost their spirit at work took responsibility for regaining it. This is true for individuals on all the paths to spirit at work, proving that we have a key role in its development.

• • • • • • •

There is no one way to experience spirit at work. No one profession has a hold on it. No one job guarantees the experience. And there is no one time in life that it occurs. Nor is it assured that once we experience spirit at work, it will always be present.

Spirit at work is a journey for most of us, and something that needs to be nurtured. There are four paths. The *always there* path has a continuous nature, whereas the *coming together* path resembles a growing and integrative path. The path to spirit at work through *transformative events* occurs as a result of an experience of spiritual awakening or a personal crisis. The path of *contextual sensitivity* is the path most dependent on the work environment.

Because we all develop spirit at work in different ways and at different stages of life, perhaps it's surprising that we experience it in similar ways, and that the experience deepens over time.

Which Path Are You On?

Take a moment to reflect on the path you are taking. Is it the path of *always there, coming together, transformative event* or *contextual sensitivity*? By identifying our path to spirit at work, we see where we need to place our attention. If we are on the *always there* path, we know that our work will take us to a deeper experience of spirit at work. If we have taken the *coming together* path, we know that our exploration will need to bring together all that is important to us. If we believe we might be on the *transformative events* path, our response to the crisis we are facing is important. And if we are on the *contextually sensitive* path, we know that our choice of employer and workplace is critical.

1. Which path to spirit at work are you on?

2. How much do the conditions of your workplace impact how you feel about your work?

3. If you are on the *always there* path, what can you do to experience spirit at work more deeply?

4. If you have gone through a personal crisis, can you see a way to turn that experience into one that puts you onto the path of spirit at work?

5. What do you know you need to do right now?

PART II

FOSTERING SPIRIT AT WORK

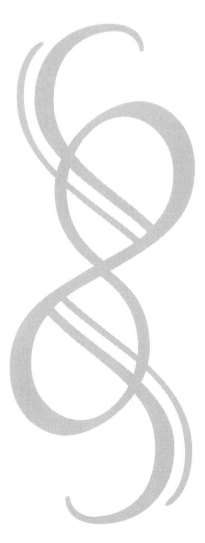

+ organization of "stress"

- reflect on your world view.

- If we play the "if only" game, we "give away our power".

The creation of spirit at work comes from within. That is not to say that organizational characteristics aren't an influence. They are. Spirit at work is a shared responsibility between the individual and organization. But people with spirit at work take responsibility and action for creating the kind of life experiences they desire, including work. They know that the power lies within. This does not mean that they do not hold the organization responsible for its part or push for better working conditions. What it means is that they *do not give away their power.*

So the question is: How do we foster spirit at work? Marsha Sinetar[8] wrote *Do What You Love, the Money Will Follow.* Doing what you love obviously makes a difference to how you feel about work. However, loving what you do can also make a powerful difference. This represents an important shift in awareness because changing one's job is not always a practical option. Nor is everyone prepared to take the leap of faith. Yet the desire for meaningful work remains. So, two ways to find meaning and fulfillment through work are by following your passion — doing what you love — or finding meaning in the work you do — loving what you do.

This part includes discussions, stories and exercises to help you get in touch with your passion and what matters to you. The larger purpose is to assist you in finding the meaning underlying your work that will help you love what you do. The next four chapters focus on actions taken by people to create or maintain spirit at work. They accomplished this by appreciating themselves and others; living purposefully and consciously; cultivating a spiritual, values-based life; and refilling their cup.

The following chapters illustrate the world views and actions of people with spirit at work through stories and exercises that personalize the message. Exercises in the accompanying guidebook are denoted with the symbol:

From my workshops, I've learned that different exercises resonate with different people. What one participant thought was worth the price of entrance, others were indifferent about. I invite you to be open to the experience afforded by the exercises, which at first glance may seem very simple but which have proven repeatedly to be powerful at influencing change.

Finally, trust yourself to know what you need at this time. If an exercise does not feel right, skip it. But don't skip it just because you think it is too easy or difficult, or because you cannot see the immediate benefit. Trust the experience of people who have found spirit at work.

One more thing. On page 197 you will find a personal planning sheet. At the end of each chapter in this section, you will be asked to identify one thing you can do to increase this experience in your life and to specify what it will take. This will help you to focus on activities with the most meaning for you and the most potential for impact. Let's get started.

chapter five

Appreciate Self and Others

What is your contribution at work? By this I mean how does your work improve the lives of others or a cause? Most of us never give this any thought. Yet if we do not appreciate who we are and how we make a difference through work, it is very unlikely that we will have spirit at work. How can we be passionate about our work if we do not recognize its value?

Spirit at work is also about relationships with ourselves, colleagues, employers and customers — and relationships with something greater than self (more about this in Chapter Seven). Earlier, I talked about how a sense of community — feelings of belonging, a shared purpose and connection with our colleagues — is an important element of spirit at work. Appreciating and valuing others and their contribution helps build and sustain a sense of community.

What Does It Mean to Be Appreciative?

To appreciate is to recognize and acknowledge the quality, value, significance or magnitude of people and things. With regard to our work, it means slowing down enough to notice and value our and others' uniqueness, strengths and contribution.

Psychologists Mitchel Adler and Nancy Fagley[9] define appreciation as "acknowledging the value and meaning of something — an event, a person, a behavior, an object — and feeling a positive emotional connection to it." So appreciating our work means understanding its value or meaning and feeling good about it. Strong connections are established and maintained through positive feelings towards ourselves and others.

Although being appreciative is often viewed as a trait we are more or less born with, these researchers also see it as something that can be developed over time. My experience is that most of us just have not taken the time to be appreciative; therefore, most of us have not experienced the reward of being appreciative.

When we are appreciative, our mood improves and we feel more connected to what we valued in the first place. Think about how appreciation can help us feel a deeper connection with ourselves, our colleagues and customers and how those connections give us a sense of belonging and shared purpose. The more appreciative we are, the more satisfied we are with our life.[10] You won't be surprised then to hear that a relationship exists between spirit at work and satisfaction with life.

In today's fast-paced world, we are losing the art of appreciation. We have been socialized to want and expect more, making it difficult to appreciate who we are and what we have. Rather than appreciating a job and what it gives us (for example, it affords us a particular lifestyle or enables us to raise our family), we often find faults and speak negatively about it. Similarly, rather than appreciate ourselves and colleagues, we tend to resort to damaging criticism.

By inviting you to become more appreciative, I am not suggesting that you ignore issues or see the world through rose-colored glasses. I am calling on you to take the time to appreciate what is.

Art of Appreciation

Appreciation can be practiced. We can take an appreciative walk or be grateful as we eat our meal or go to sleep in our warm beds at night. As we practice noticing and being thankful for what is around us, we are in a better position to appreciate ourselves and others.

This will pave the way to appreciating ourselves and our contribution as well as those of our colleagues. Respecting our own worth, respecting the value of others, connecting from the heart and practicing accountability are ways to appreciate ourselves and others, and that contributes to spirit at work.

Give Yourself a Little Respect

Kids Are Worth It and So Are You

Barbara Coloroso,[11] internationally recognized speaker and author, taught the world that "kids are worth it" and that good parenting begins with treating kids with dignity and respect. Appreciating self starts by treating ourselves with dignity and respect, and recognizing and valuing our own worth. Self-respect is of great importance to our everyday life and our experience of spirit at work. It is essential to live a satisfying, meaningful, fulfilling life — a life worth living. But we can't be given self-respect; it comes from within.

When I first started to deliver spirit-at-work workshops, I heard a woman say, "I am just a secretary." I couldn't believe that that was how she viewed herself: as "just a." Everyone knows it is the administrative support staff that keeps the organization running and without them, the rest of us would be toast. Administrative support staff know where everyone is and how to locate them. They are who we go to when we need to see the boss. Need a form? They know which one, where it is and how to complete it. Computer just froze? Who do you turn to for help? Need something typed up in a hurry, an appointment made, a meeting booked with several different departments? You get the message. We know it, but sadly, most administrative support people do not.

I often tell this story at staff retreats. And, when I do, the non-administrative staff immediately begin nodding their heads in agreement. They know exactly what I am talking about. As a sign of recognition, many of them begin to clap, at which point the administrative support staff go into shock. They have a hard time believing that others know and appreciate how important their work is. And how important they are to the success of the business. They have real difficulty believing in their value.

Like the secretary, most of us do not respect or value our worth. We do not see how our work helps anyone or anything. We often feel we are spinning our wheels, putting out fires or putting in time. Rather than valuing our work, we might be embarrassed by it and its seeming lack of importance, which leads to feelings of disrespect. One way of changing this is to become clear about our unique contribution at work.

What Is Your Unique Contribution at Work?

What do you bring to your work that is unique to you? What are your strengths? Abilities? Skills? What are you known for? Why do colleagues seek you out? What would be missed if you no longer worked at your organization? Take a moment and create a list of your attributes. Write down the positive things that others have said about you or that you would like them to have noticed. Recall the compliments you have received. Remember the times you were proud — what made you proud? List your accomplishments — what made them accomplishments?

These attributes might be *personality characteristics,* e.g., helpful to others, cheery disposition, conscientious. They might be *interpersonal skills and abilities,* e.g., friendly with and respectful of customers and clients, problem-solving and conflict management abilities, a clear communicator. Perhaps they're *leadership skills,* e.g., visionary, a sound decision maker, skilled planner. There's also *content expertise,* e.g., highly trained in a particular area, financial expertise. Or *technical abilities,* e.g., runs great meetings, able to operate sophisticated equipment and technology, specialized training. What is it that only you can do?

The Appreciating Yourself at Work exercise will help you do just that. I must warn you: Many people find this a difficult task to complete. Please stick with it. The harder it is to do, the more value it will likely have. Many women and people in the helping professions are particularly challenged by this exercise, probably because they are trained to be caregivers and not take credit for what they do. Others tell me that they were brought up not to boast. This is not about bragging; it is about recognizing your special skills and abilities and what you have to offer others. It is about appreciating yourself and your work.

Appreciate the Significance of Your Work

All work has value. All work matters. All work gives us the opportunity to make a contribution. But sometimes we have to see beyond the seemingly meaningless aspect of our work to appreciate this. I call this "seemingly meaningless" because at first glance, it may be difficult to find the meaning underlying some work. But every job holds the power to make a difference and enable each employee to experience spirit at work. I would like to share a story about Hien.

Hien was an accountant prior to immigrating to Canada, but the professional association for accountants did not accept her qualifications. She was forced to find work in another field. Hien became a nursing attendant in long-term care. While she felt good about working and providing for her family, Hien did not feel proud of her work. More than that, she was embarrassed. She saw herself as a "bum washer." With a label like that, how could she ever appreciate the contribution she made?

It was only through exploring how her work mattered to others that Hien was able to gain some appreciation of her work. As she came to understand what it must feel like for the previously independent residents to be completely dependent on others for their personal and private care, and how wonderful it must feel to be cleaned up, Hien began to see the value of her work.

As she thought further about the gift she was giving to the residents' relatives (likely their busy adult children), she realized that, yes, what she did mattered. What really drove the point home was thinking about what it would be like if that resident were her mother or father. At last, Hien understood why her work mattered. She was able to value her work and feel good about what she was doing.

The following exercise will help you uncover why your work matters. Using the information from the previous exercise, write down one contribution you make through your work. Then write about why that is important to you and why doing something important matters to you. Then keep asking yourself, "And why does that matter?" until you feel an emotional response.

At first glance, it might seem you are being asked to repeat yourself, but in actual fact, the questioning allows you to go deeper and deeper until you get to the essence of the importance of your work.

If, after a while, you are not moved by what you have written, keep asking yourself the question, "And why does that matter?" until you are moved emotionally. If you are moved to tears, you know that you have uncovered the essence of your work. Some of us might create fifty to 100 reasons why work matters. But when we look at the list, we see a recurring theme. Circle the themes and see if you can create a statement about why your work matters that resonates with you.

It often takes more than three or four tries to get to this deeper essence, but when you do, it is generally an "aha!" moment and you will view your work differently from this point forward.

For some people, this exercise is life-altering. Their view of work is transformed, and all because they were able to get to its essence or higher purpose. Given an opportunity to explore why our work matters, most of us are able to understand and appreciate the deeper meaning and thus the contribution we make. The key is to understand why it matters to *us*. Others may see value in what we are doing, but to achieve spirit at work, we must see the value ourselves. Spirit at work requires this alignment between what we do and how we view it.

In addition to helping us appreciate ourselves and our work, this new knowledge opens up a realm of possibilities. Many of us are able to gain clarity about our "mission" in life and how work helps us achieve it. Once we have this awareness, and especially when the going gets rough, we can use it to remind ourselves why we chose or stay with this particular work. Finally, we can use this new information to keep us on track by facilitating choices, making decisions and directing the order of work.

Show Others Respect

They Are Worth It, Too

Kids are worth it, you are worth it and so are your colleagues and supervisors. We all deserve to be treated with dignity and respect. Everyone has value and everyone brings something to the organization. The key is to uncover what that is. For co-workers we like, the task is simple. For others, we need to dig a little deeper.

Aretha Franklin told us in 1967 that it all begins with a little R-E-S-P-E-C-T. There's the type of respect that involves behavior and the kind described as an attitude or feeling. Of course, attitude and action do not always go hand in hand. It is possible to act in ways that appear respectful even as we feel disrespect, as in when we say the politically correct thing but do not mean it. Unfortunately, attitudes and feelings carry more weight than actions. The good news is that when we have a positive attitude and intend respect, the actions that follow also tend to be positive.

What does being respectful mean to you? In general, to respect someone is to appreciate and take into consideration their feelings, needs, thoughts, ideas, desires and preferences. To show respect is to attach value and worth to another person and their point of view. It is about showing tolerance, acceptance and common decency towards the people around us — our colleagues, supervisors, leaders, staff, customers, clients, people older or younger than us and people from different walks of life.

Where do we start? Can you recall a time when someone showed you respect for something you said or did? How did it feel? How did he or she let you know that you were respected and appreciated? How might you use this information to show respect towards others?

Our intent, followed by positive actions, will result in more positive feelings about the people around us. While intent is a very important first step, it is not enough. We need to act on our intent. So let us think respect *and* be respectful.

Recognize Their Contribution

It tends to be easier to respect and appreciate others when we value their roles. Just as we did for ourselves, it is important to understand the unique contribution of others. What do they bring that is helpful, creative or different? What is it about their work that matters?

Often we spend too much time looking for similarities and get annoyed with differences. Yet if we were all alike, the organization would have gaping holes. Can you imagine if everyone wanted to be on the social committee and arrange parties, potlucks and celebrations? Or if everyone was detail oriented and analytical and determined to go through every line of a document? Or if everyone liked to do sales, but no one was good at maintenance? I suspect that the company would quickly find itself in trouble. Yet, we get annoyed when the number crunchers ask for more data to substantiate our request for more money to operate programs. The number crunchers are disappointed because we don't appreciate the added value they bring.

What is the answer? Understand how your colleagues make a contribution and why their work matters. Maybe Gloria down the hall doesn't always respond to her emails in a timely fashion, but she sure makes sure that we get together on a regular basis. Could it be because of her that we have a strong sense of team? It might seem like Alan in finance doesn't care about the programs we offer, but he keeps on top of the budget and makes sure we have enough money to honor our commitments. Maybe Alan does care about the work we do, but he knows his best contribution is to ensure there is enough money.

Take a moment and think about the people you work with. What are their strengths? Contributions? What is it about their contributions that matters? Then begin, each day, to show your appreciation towards your colleagues and supervisors. Tell them why their contributions matter to you and to the company.

Show Your Appreciation

How might you show appreciation? The simple things carry the greatest impact. Recognize and acknowledge people as individuals; recognize and acknowledge their particular contributions. The list below compiles ideas developed during my workshops:

Say thanks; show gratitude.

- Verbalize appreciation for the contribution of others.

- Send thank-you notes.

- Acknowledge each other's strengths, expertise, skills and abilities.

- Put up a "bragging board." Post notes of thanks from clients, customers and colleagues.

Practice active listening with others.

- Be present and give your full attention when in conversation or working together.

- Check out assumptions, especially negative ones.

- Get curious about your colleagues — get to know them.

Show compassion.

- Be observant — appreciate the situations of others.
- Respond appropriately and give each other a little leeway.
- Help out others with or without being asked.

Be inclusive of others.

- Include all members of the team.
- Invite the ideas of others.
- Share social activities; eat together.

Show respect.

- Appreciate diversity.
- Be non-judgmental.
- Treat everyone in every position with dignity.
- Weigh the consequences of your behavior on others.

Be kind.

- Show interest in others; learn about one another's profession.
- Send anonymous words of encouragement.
- Pay it forward — when someone has shown you kindness, pay it forward by showing appreciation or kindness to others.

Celebrate big and little things.

- Find reasons to celebrate.
- Recognize life events of others.
- Pause and reflect on the contribution others have made.

Connect from the Heart

For most, spirit at work is strongest when they connect with others from the heart. We get out of our heads (and judgment) and get interested in our colleagues, clients and customers. We take time to talk to them, to get to know them. As we build relationships, we treat them the way they want to be treated. We care about them and show it. We treat them like family.

Get Interested in Others at Work

Too often we choose to ignore or separate ourselves from people we don't understand or to whom we've failed to connect. And yet, a way to become connected is to get to know the person. Get interested. Become curious. Who are they? What are their interests? What do they do when they are not working? What are they passionate about? What are their life goals? What is interesting about them? What is it about this work that attracted them to their job?

Diversity at work is natural, maybe even desirable. In fact, evidence indicates that diversity results in increased creativity at work. But it can bring with it a number of problems, such as divisiveness and conflict. While we're familiar with cultural diversity, we also face moral, sexual, religious, occupational and age diversity. Never before have we experienced four generations of employees in the labor market at the same time, each with its own point of view, values and expectations. It seems to me that we have no choice, especially if we want to experience spirit at work, but to get to know one another and to appreciate one another, including our differences.

I once worked with a team of multicultural staff who were at odds with one another. Groups formed, boundaries were drawn, and gossip ran rampant. Feelings were hurt, anger increased, and the cliques grew stronger. There was no connection, no common purpose. The situation impacted work to the point that it put patients at risk.

In addition to doing exercises included in this book, I asked each person to become mindful of what was important to them, what mattered in their lives and what they wanted to bring more of into their lives. Over a period of two months, their assignment was to collect pictures, quotes, objects, anything that represented these things, and to create a vision board. The object was to emerge with something concrete that represented and reminded participants of what was important and what they wanted to focus on day to day. As part of our celebration at the end of the two months, I asked each person to share what they had created with their colleagues. While not everyone chose to share, everyone showed up to listen to their colleagues' presentations.

I cannot begin to tell you how powerful this was. Each person took a turn, showing their pictures or objects and speaking from the heart about what was important. In sharing what mattered to them, they also shared their stories. And as they shared their stories, the walls between them began to come down. They started to realize what they had in common — they were parents, children, wives, husbands with similar fears, hopes and dreams — and they had more in common than they had differences. Their hearts went out to their colleagues as they heard about difficulties experienced coming to this new country in search of a better life for themselves and their children, and the challenges they still faced trying to fit in. Divisiveness turned into compassion because they were connected from the heart. And when we are connected from the heart, it becomes easier to treat our colleagues like family.

Treat Them Like Family

Many parents channel their children, especially boys, into sports so they can work off aggression. Working off aggression is one thing; working out aggression is another. For a time, my son played football, which is a rough sport. I'd have preferred he not play, but how do you deny someone his passion? And once you agree to him playing, how can you not support him? So I went to his games, and as I sat in the bleachers, I became conflicted by what I saw, heard and felt.

These kids hurt one another, and it is all seen as part of the sport. "It is football," parents would tell me as they cheered on our team. "That is what they are supposed to do." We had a tough season and didn't win many games, but one afternoon, everything was different. We had the upper hand and were winning. We were bigger, stronger, faster. At last, the scoreboard was in our favor.

I was supposed to be happy, but all I could see was the other team's players getting hurt. One had to be taken off the field in an ambulance.

The look on the faces of the parents of the opposing team said it all. I saw clearly that something was wrong. How could one set of parents be cheering their children on while the other set of parents was holding their breath and hoping that their children didn't get hurt? Weren't we all parents? Didn't we all love our children equally? Didn't we all want what was best for our children? How could we share these desires and simultaneously be happy when they hurt one another?

A similar situation often happens at work. We form groups: us and them. We become critical and judgmental of "them" and accepting and supportive of "us." Differences grow and separate us. Either you are in or you are out. We forget that we are all working towards a common goal and that we all have something to contribute.

What would happen if we treated our colleagues like family? Would anything change? Most of us agree that even if we aren't best friends with family members or don't always see eye to eye, we will be there in a flash if they need us. Why? They are family and that is what families do. There is a connection.

This connection promotes tolerance of family members who are overly talkative, loud, continuously late, judgmental, dress funny or have different political or religious views than us. We realize this is only part of who they are. We know and appreciate the other parts. We focus on their strengths and hopefully ignore the differences. After several political arguments with Uncle Frank, we come to accept that we have different philosophical views and stop talking about politics. We find commonalities. We get interested.

The same is true with our colleagues. They are real people. Just like us, they have feelings. They have hopes and dreams and families they care about. They have strengths. They have annoying behaviors. Just like us, they are human. What if we began to look for commonalities and became interested? What if we treated them like family?

Shift to the Platinum Rule

Most of us are familiar with the Golden Rule, "Do unto others as you would have them do unto you." While the intent is honorable, the idea of treating others as you would like to be treated assumes that you and the other person are the same. And we know that simply isn't the case.

I learned this very early on in my marriage. My husband Fred is more of a "be-er" and I am more of a "do-er." We are both able to shift from being to doing and doing to being, but we definitely have our preferences, which have a way of coming out when we are under pressure. We couldn't figure out why we were unsuccessful in supporting one another during stressful times. Rather than assisting one another, it seemed that our efforts contributed to the frustration. It took us a while to learn that we were practicing the Golden Rule and it was not working.

When I observed that Fred was under pressure or had a hard day at the office, I went into action. I started "doing" things to help. I tried to take things off his plate, make him a nice meal, take over responsibilities to free him up. It didn't work. I couldn't figure it out, so I started working harder and doing more things. It only added to the upset.

Stress also rose between us when I seemed to have too much to do or felt overwhelmed. Instead of going into action, Fred gave me a hug and wanted to sit down and talk about what it was that was bothering me. I couldn't believe it. How could I possibly sit down and talk when I was already behind and had so much to do? I didn't get how he didn't get it. The truth is, neither of us "got it."

We were practicing the Golden Rule. We were doing for each other what it was we would have liked the other to do for us. I was going into action, but Fred wanted me to sit and listen. Fred wanted to sit and listen, but I wanted him to help out — to take some of the work off my plate. No wonder it didn't work.

What we needed was the Platinum Rule,[12] "Do unto others as they'd like done unto them." This requires that we think about what the other person would like before we act. These days, I know that if Fred is tired or under pressure, what he needs from me is a listening ear, and when I am overwhelmed, he knows that I need some help to get the work or project done.

The Platinum Rule also applies at work. Take the time to get to know your colleagues well enough to know what they need. Better yet, ask them how you can best be of assistance — then follow through. Treat them as they would like to be treated.

Show Up and Be Responsible

Life is full of choices. Being responsible means being in charge of our choices and by extension our experiences in life, including those at work. Being responsible also means recognizing that our actions matter — both to ourselves and those around us. Being accountable means that we are on the hook for the consequences of those actions. Practicing responsibility and accountability are two important ways to demonstrate appreciation for ourselves and others.

Practice Accountability

Accountability is about integrity and character. It is about doing the best job we can and accepting responsibility for any oversights or errors we make along the way. When we are accountable, we meet our commitments despite how challenging or complicated life gets.

We are all familiar with being accountable to others, but accountability is a two-way street. This means we follow through with commitments to *ourselves* and colleagues, the people we serve, our organization, etc. As we become more connected to others from the heart, it becomes easier and more desirable to become accountable towards others.

> Sandra was a police officer who didn't particularly like doing paperwork. She didn't see the connection between writing reports and helping others. More than that, she felt she wasn't really doing her job of taking care of society when she was behind a desk writing.
>
> One day, however, it became clear that people were waiting for her report in order to get important matters dealt with. They could not bring a home invasion case to conclusion until she had finalized her report. At that moment, Sandra realized that report writing mattered and completing these reports meant being accountable to those she served. She began to view this component of her work in a completely different way.

Accountability is all about ownership: owning our work, decisions, successes and failures. Holding ourselves accountable helps us take pride in what we do. Being accountable gives us the energy we need to do quality work that enriches the lives of our co-workers and clients.

Accountability is the foundation of collaboration, trust and team building. Increased respect and camaraderie and less frustration and upset result when team members are accountable to one another.

Do What You Say You Are Going to Do

People like to count on others doing what they say they are going to do. Yet stuff happens. Extra assignments come in. Delays in orders prevent us from meeting deadlines. Colleagues don't meet their deadlines. Kids get sick. Emergencies arise. Sometimes things just don't work out as planned. Life happens. Even so, people want to know they can usually rely on you.

Some of us are people pleasers and agree to anything we are asked to do, including unreasonable expectations or timelines. Then we find ourselves squeezed trying to meet them. Some of us realize the impossibility of achieving the expectation and just drop it, bearing the brunt of the consequences. Others do anything necessary to meet the expectation, including letting go of accountability towards themselves and family. What is your response to these situations? And how has that worked out for you?

Part of being accountable to ourselves is taking the time to ensure that our response considers all our commitments — to ourself, family, other customers and other projects. Here are some accountability tips:

1. *Gain clarity about the expectation.* Take time to understand the scope of the request and the time likely required to fulfill it before making a commitment.
2. *Avoid unwise commitments.* Prior to agreeing to the commitment, decide whether you are willing and likely to keep it. Are there other commitments or future events that could make it difficult or impossible to meet this request?
3. *Assess this request against your other commitments.* What are the consequences of accepting this commitment to your existing commitments?
4. *Do your best.* Once you commit, choose to do your best; choose to be reliable and diligent.
5. *Avoid excuses.* Finish what you start, overcoming obstacles if necessary. Avoid excuses such as "That is just the way I am,"

"There never was enough time to do this assignment properly," "This is how it is done around here" or "It wasn't my job."

6. *Adopt an attitude of "the buck stops here."* Don't look for someone else to blame or to pass the issue on to. Take responsibility and, as the Nike slogan says, "Just do it."

7. *Adopt a kaizen approach.* For example, strive for continuous improvement in all aspects of your life and work. Look for ways to do your work better.

8. *Keep others in the loop.* Provide periodic updates, including early warning signals.

9. *Seek assistance.* Stuff happens. If it becomes clear that you are unable to meet the commitment, seek the assistance of others about the best steps to take. Ask for help earlier rather than later.

10. *Deliver on commitments.* Do what you say you will do.

Accountability means commitment and that is a little scary for some of us. But once we choose to be accountable and follow these accountability tips, we will be clear about whether each expectation is an appropriate commitment for us and whether we can meet it. This puts us in a position to make a conscious choice. Where we don't actually have a choice to accept the assignment, it will give us the information we need to negotiate or at least give a heads-up about competing priorities to our superiors. Once we accept, the rest of the tips will support us to meet our commitment and feel good about what we are doing. After all, that is what this is all about, right? If we are going to do it, we may as well feel good about it.

Show Others How to Treat You

How are you teaching others about how to treat you? As people get to know us, whether in our personal lives or at work, they learn how they can or cannot treat us. The behaviors we tolerate from others are considered acceptable and become more difficult to change over time. Most of the time these interactions happen unconsciously, but the interaction is working perfectly. Have you ever experienced something like this?

Mike was a salesman for a large oil and gas company. His boss, John, had a habit of losing his cool when under stress. Mike liked John and knew he was under a lot of pressure to meet deadlines, so gave him some slack. "After all, he's not really hurting anyone," Mike thought. "He's just letting off a little steam."

One morning, Mike heard John screaming at one of Mike's colleagues over the phone. This was the first time he'd heard John's anger directed towards another person. Mike quietly walked down the hall and closed John's office door. He hoped John would get the hint without his having to say anything. A few days later, John came into Mike's office to talk about a project that was overdue. Mike was looking forward to the discussion because he felt he was at a stalemate and couldn't move forward without John's input. Also, Mike had put the project on hold when given other assignments with a higher priority.

As Mike began to explain the situation, he noticed John sighing and looking out the window. Mike ignored the cues and proceeded to outline the roadblocks in the project — at which point John lost it. He began to put Mike down and say that as a friend, he'd thought he could count on Mike to get the job done. His booming voice carried throughout the department. Mike was thankful most of his co-workers had already left for lunch. He felt humiliated. Shocked that John would holler at him like that, Mike wasn't sure what to do. So he did nothing. Over the next few days, he began to feel uncomfortable working near John, never knowing what would happen next.

Soon after, Mike and John were at a team meeting with seven of Mike's colleagues. As everyone gave an update, Mike could see John becoming agitated. His face was flushed, he tapped his feet, and he constantly interrupted. Mike began to sweat. Surely John wasn't going to lose it again, not in public. Well, he did. And who do you think it was directed towards? The person who'd tolerated this behavior up until recently and who, through his non-action, had unconsciously given John permission to continue to treat him this way.

We teach others how to treat us. Mike thought that he was being supportive of John and giving him some slack, but in essence, he was saying that it was okay for Mike to holler at him, including in public. Maybe Mike thought it was okay for bosses to shout at employees. Maybe he felt employees should not speak out about such behavior to a boss. Maybe Mike felt guilty or embarrassed for disappointing John. There are a host of reasons as to why someone like Mike might accept someone like John's behavior. But the bottom line is that by letting it continue, he was saying non-verbally that John's behavior was acceptable.

We do this all the time. And then we get upset with the results. I am not saying it is easy to stand up to such treatment, but it is necessary. It shows others how to treat us. What might Mike have done differently?

- After John had time to cool down from the phone call, Mike could have talked to him. He could have said, "Sounds like that was a pretty tough call. What is happening?" or "Are things okay? I haven't heard you get upset like that before." Both examples would have let John know his behavior had been noticed, that Mike was concerned and that Mike was offering a listening ear.

- In the incident in Mike's office, Mike might have responded to John's early cues. "Are you alright, John? You don't seem to be your regular self these days. How about you and I go for lunch?"

- Having missed those cues, Mike could have responded to John's shouting in the following ways. He could have stood up, put his hand on John's shoulder and said, "Sounds like you have a lot on your plate right now. What can I do to help?" or "You seem to be under a lot of pressure these days. How is it going?"

- If John didn't respond positively to those phrases, Mike could have said, "It seems like this conversation is very upsetting to you. How about we continue our talk later this afternoon?"

- If John kept it up but refused to schedule another time, Mike could have said, "John, I know that this is troubling you and you are upset with what I have done (or not done), but I cannot continue this conversation if you shout. Can you lower your voice or shall we find another time to meet?"

- And if that didn't work, Mike might have said, "I am going to have to have this conversation with you later" and left the office.

- It is more difficult to take on your boss in public. During the team meeting, it would have been best for Mike to let John let off some steam, try to divert the conversation, suggest a break or find a way to remove himself until John calmed down. Taking John on in public would likely have just upped the ante. And the boss always seems to win.

- After the meeting and when John had a chance to calm down, Mike could have spoken to John, one-on-one. Mike could then again have asked John what was happening. He could have shared his observations (dates, times and incidents) and expressed concern about John's changed behavior. He could have told John what it felt like when John was shouting and saying he wasn't okay with that behavior in the future. He could have asked John how they might deal with it differently next time.

Our beliefs about ourselves underlie how we act and show others the way to treat us. As we become more accountable to ourselves, we take personal responsibility to teach others about our boundaries and how to respect us. It becomes easier to show others how to behave towards us in positive ways when we appreciate who we are and respect our own worth.

The act of appreciating self and others translates into respecting our own worth, respecting the value of others, connecting from the heart, nurturing relationships and practicing accountability.

1. What do you appreciate most about yourself?

2. What is your unique contribution at work?

3. How will showing appreciation to others enhance your spirit at work?

4. What would happen if you began to treat your colleagues like family?

5. What does it mean to be accountable to self?

6. How accountable are you to others at work?

7. How can you show others how to treat you differently?

8. What one thing might you do differently? What would it take? (Record on page 197)

chapter six

Live Purposefully and Consciously

A powerful way to foster spirit at work and enhance our work experiences is to live purposefully and consciously. We do this through *conscious intent* — being mindful about how we live our lives and choosing to live with purpose and meaning.

To be "conscious" is to be aware, alert, mindful, cognizant, reflective and deliberate. "Intent" refers to our objective, purpose, aim or plan. Hence, *conscious intent* is about being aware of our intent or purpose, being cognizant about the choices we make and being mindful of the meaning and consequences of our action.

Without action, intent — whether it is conscious or not — has little meaning. I may intend to return the call of an upset client. I might even be very conscious of the importance of quickly correcting the error our business created — even though I am extremely busy with other customers. My thought or intent may be honorable, but without the action, it carries little meaning. Not many customers or clients will feel satisfied that we "thought" about them and their concern. They want to see action.

Living purposefully distinguishes people with spirit at work from those without it. Those with spirit at work practice conscious intent on which they take action.

Living purposefully and consciously is an art. It involves knowing yourself, being intentional, feeling integrated, being aware of the power of thought and choosing consciously. We will explore each of these elements in this chapter.

Know Yourself

What is my deeper purpose? Before I can answer this question, I must first get to know myself. I must pause and pay attention, be mindful, and become a witness to my life.

—Frank, regional coordinator

In order to live consciously and purposefully, we must know who we are, what is important to us and what moves our heart. We must also know what we stand for and our deeper reason for being. People with spirit at work practice mindfulness and use it to pursue self-awareness. They engage in a continual process of discernment, reflection and self-examination to determine what gives them personal meaning. They explore their personal values, belief systems and interests. They seek clarity about their personal mission, life direction or purpose in life, which is beyond self. Once they determine their purpose, they examine how they can live out this purpose and, in particular, how their work contributes to that purpose. On a regular basis (daily for some), these individuals evaluate the relationship between their day-to-day living and what gives them meaning and feels good. Ben, the physiotherapist, says we need to ask ourselves, "Is what I am doing on a daily basis fulfilling? Is it nurturing me? Is it a part of what I want to accomplish in my life?"

What follows is a discussion about how people with spirit at work live purposefully by increasing their awareness of self. Each section includes at least one idea to help you become more aware of what gives you meaning. Further exercises can be found in the companion guidebook.

Be Mindful

We frequently go through our day-to-day actions on autopilot. Not thinking. Not being aware of what is happening around us. Zoning out or not paying attention. Shutting down the inputs because we have reached our capacity. We often lose the present moment because we are thinking about the future or worrying about something that happened in the past. In doing so, we miss the gifts of the present — a smile, the beauty of a flower, the warmth of a touch or the gift of kindness.

When we are caught up in thoughts or worries, we are effectively absent from our body. No one is home. We might be walking by a beautiful garden, but we cannot see the flowers. We can be served a delicious meal, but we do not taste it. Our loved ones may be sending us strong cues, but we do not hear them. We are preoccupied. But by shifting our attention to the present moment — to our breathing, walking and surroundings — we come back into our body and become aware.

Mindfulness is about paying attention on purpose. Noticing in a non-judgmental way. Being present. Living in the moment. Being aware. Giving 100 percent attention to what we are doing. It is about tasting the food we eat, smelling the scents of the out-of-doors, seeing the beauty in the everyday. It is about being present with our customers, clients, colleagues, friends and family members. Being in touch with their needs.

Being mindful involves quieting the mind and practicing stillness in order to create space for a deeper way of knowing, and increasing awareness of self and what matters. Thus, to be mindful is to observe self or as Wayne Dyer[13] calls it, to witness one's life. As we become an observer, we gain clarity about our unique purpose.

Being mindful is a way to access our own resources for growing, healing and self-compassion. Mindfulness provides access to the inner wisdom required to create the kind of life we wish to lead. Moreover, it is a practical way to get in touch with our authentic self. It involves self-observation and self-inquiry.

So, we want to shift our attention to the present moment and the nuances around us. We want to use all our senses, taking time to taste and smell, hear and see, touch and feel. We want to take the time to feel our connectedness with all things.

Mindfulness reflection. In what ways have you been mindful? Examples might include paying attention to the taste and texture of the foods you eat, being present and fully listening to a colleague or friend as they talk, or thinking carefully before speaking so that your message will be heard. Maybe it is listening to sounds, smelling smells and seeing the sights around you. We've all experienced mindfulness. Take a moment to remind yourself how it felt to be present, open and aware. What could you do to be more mindful?

Pause and Pay Attention

Take a five-minute walk. Inside or outside. Your task is to observe. To be mindful. To notice. To pause and pay attention. Sights. Smells. Sounds. Touch. Taste. Feelings. As you walk around, see these things through the eyes of a child, as if you were seeing them for the first time. See with wonder, delight and absorption. This is mindfulness, or moment-by-moment, non-judgmental awareness. Come back and jot down what the experience was like and what you noticed.

I find that people are often very surprised at what they observe, especially if they apply the exercise in a familiar territory like their workplace. One group of employees was shocked to notice pictures on walls they had been walking past for years. Others were surprised to actually observe the route they took to work. They could not believe the scenery they had been missing. Rather than view the drive to work as drudgery, one person began to look forward to the changing fall colors. One woman had never before noticed a scent in her workplace. All this because they took the time to notice. To be mindful.

Whenever you have a moment, pause and pay attention. Practice mindful eating. As you eat your meal, become fully conscious of the smell and taste of your food. Be aware of the color. Feel the texture. Notice what happens as you chew the food, feel it move from your mouth down through your throat to your stomach. Take time to pause and pay attention to everyday tasks like gardening, grocery shopping, washing dishes. Use the opportunity of being stuck in traffic to breathe and notice your surroundings. What is the scenery? What colors are new vehicles? What songs are playing on the radio? Think of it — you don't have anything to do but be. Enjoy the moment. If you phone someone and are put on hold, close your eyes and become aware of your body. Notice any tension you might be holding and release it. Observe your breath. Choose to use the few minutes that on-hold status has given you. Give thanks for the opportunity to pause and pay attention.

• • • • • • •

Complete books are devoted to mindfulness,[14] and I encourage you to explore them. Mindfulness promotes a whole host of positive outcomes. For our purposes, it's useful because it helps us get in touch with what is important to us. To understand the things that matter.

Know What Matters

It is impossible to live consciously and purposefully without knowing what is important. By engaging in a continual process of discernment, reflection and self-examination, we can determine what gives us meaning. Once we have clarity about what is important, we are in a position to live with intent and experience spirit at work. The following exercises approach the questions "What matters most to me?" and "What is my deeper purpose?" in different ways. At the end of this section, you will be in a position to write a purpose or mission statement.

Become a Witness

To become a witness is to become an observer of your own life. To watch. To listen. To hear. To feel. Over the next six weeks, I am inviting you to become a witness to your life. This exercise is not limited to work. Your assignment is to observe and notice: What gives you meaning? Joy? What inspires you? Energizes you? Excites you? What is your purpose? When do you feel proud? What rewards do you get from work? When are you happiest? Most fulfilled? Feeling like you are making a difference?

As you begin to notice, collect objects, pictures, phrases or stories that represent what gives you meaning. Write poetry, draw pictures, take photographs or collect symbols. The act of witnessing becomes a creative act, so choose a method that moves you. You will quickly notice yourself becoming more mindful. Flipping through a magazine becomes a whole new experience. The pictures begin to hold meaning. They strike a chord with you. You begin to think about what is important and how you want to be spending your time. Observe (without judgment) and continue to collect.

Set aside an hour at the end of the six weeks. Mark it on your calendar and call it a date with self. Use the time to pull your material together and select a way to display it. For example, if you collected pictures, you may choose to paste them on a poster board. If you collected items, you may wish to find a special container for them. Once they're displayed, reflect on their importance. Ponder how each came to be part of your collection. Now take a moment to create a list of the things that matter to you. We will come back to this list later.

When I first did this exercise, I created a collage of pictures, phrases and quotes to which I added symbolic items. For example, in addition to the pictures of family, beautiful gardens, newspaper clippings and inspirational quotes, I included a feather to represent nature, a doll's lounger to represent the importance of taking care of myself, and a small plant pot to symbolize gardening. These items did not mean I was actually doing a good job of taking care of myself or that I was doing as much gardening as I wanted to; they just symbolized the importance of these things to me. Recall that mindfulness is to be aware, but without judgment.

Have your collection or collage visible, as it is an instant reminder of what you decided was important. You will be surprised how this simple collection will help you live purposefully and consciously. My poster hangs in my office and is a good reminder that things besides work are important. I love my work. So it is easy to get carried away and forget about the other matters also important to me. Often, after getting a glimpse of my poster, I choose to do something other than work. I am reminded that what we focus our attention on grows stronger.

Personal invitation. When you return to work, practice witnessing or observing your day-to-day activities. What effect does witnessing yourself in action have on the way you work, how you feel about your work, your relationships with customers or clients, your relationships with colleagues and how you interact with others? Expect to find a change in how you feel, in your relationships and interactions.

Clarify Your Values

Clarifying values is another way to uncover deeper meaning. I like to think of a value as a principle, conviction or standard that guides our behaviors. Rokeach[15] differentiates between terminal and instrumental values. Terminal values can be thought of as personal goals we want to achieve during our lifetime (e.g., a sense of accomplishment, freedom, inner harmony, family security, health). Instrumental values can be seen as ways of achieving these goals (e.g., ambitious, courageous, helpful, honest, responsible). The terminal and instrumental values we hold dear are reflected in how we see the world, the commitments we make and the actions we take.

What is your world view? Earlier, I pointed out that behavior is aligned with intent. It is also aligned with values and belief systems. All our actions stem from our values and world view. Every decision we make can be traced back to our values, beliefs, maybe even culture. How we spend our time, who we spend it with, where we work, how we work and where we spend our money — these are all influenced by our values. How would you describe your belief system? Is the universe friendly or not? Are people mostly good or bad? Selfish or helpful? Do you see the glass as half empty or half full?

Competing values. Our commitments also reflect values. However, sometimes we say we are committed to one thing but do another. For example, we may say that we are committed to family and yet we miss all the family functions due to work. We may say that we are committed to getting into shape, but do not work out. We may say that we are committed to saving money, but spend our earnings on a new car. Choosing to work, not working out and buying a new car are secondary commitments that reflect values. The only problem is that fulfilling these secondary commitments often undermines primary values and commitments. When commitments are contradictory, they create tension. They are competing values.[16]

These secondary values could be called "shadow values" because they lurk in the dark. We might not even be aware of them, but they are very powerful, sometimes more powerful than our first layer of values. Because of that, we need to bring them into the light.

By bringing shadow values into the light, we begin to understand our behaviors more fully. We begin to realize that our behaviors are congruent with our values. The employee who misses all the family functions may be more committed to being accepted by colleagues, so stays late to finish a product. The individual who says she is committed to getting into shape may also be committed to retaining her friends, and they just happen to despise working out. The person who believes he is committed to saving money may also be committed to ensuring that his pregnant wife has a reliable vehicle.

Our behaviors are expressions of a bigger purpose with which we are rarely in touch. So if we are not following through with something we claim to value, we need to look deeper to understand the competing value. Competing values are often based on fears — for example, the need for security or acceptance, fear of change or fear of inadequacy. This is the case in both our personal and professional lives. Understanding these "shadow values" gives us clarity about why we sometimes do not stand up for things we say we are committed to. What are your competing values? How do they impact choices you make at work?

Values also change over time and with age. Different values take priority at different stages of life. Values also change in response to crisis situations. For example, most people who go through a near-death experience undergo a profound personality transformation.[17] The values of Americans differed after the 2001 September 11th terrorist attack. After the attack, values related to survival and safety increased, and values related to self-esteem and self-actualization (that sense of accomplishment and self-respect) decreased. This is consistent with Maslow's hierarchy of needs, and particularly the need for safety first. A parallel change in values occurs during a recession. Similarly, tragedies such as the loss of a loved one, being diagnosed with a terminal disease or confronting difficult life situations like divorce or job loss often lead us to re-evaluate and reprioritize our values.

Clarifying our values enables us to put our energy towards what matters most to us. Of the several ways a person can clarify their values, I find completing a "values sort" to be very quick and effective.

What values do you hold dear? Which one would you identify as your signature value — the one that defines you? How do you live it? How do you bring it into your life? To your work? What stands in the way of you fulfilling this value? What other values do you carry that compete with your signature value? Is there anything you need in order to honor this value?

Values matter. They are a part of our identity. They also help form our belief system: If I hold this value, then I can expect something to happen. I call this the *If Game*. Here are some examples:

Example 1. If I have a *sense of accomplishment,* then I will feel good about myself. And that matters because I was always told that I wouldn't make anything out of myself. When I feel a sense of accomplishment, I know I am worthy and I can do things.

Example 2. If I am *helpful,* then other people can achieve their goals. And that matters because I want to be of service to others. I feel like my work is of value when I see other people benefiting. I am not just here for the money; I want to make a difference.

Example 3. If I have my *health,* then I can do anything! And that is important to me because I am a single parent and my family relies on me. I want to make sure that I can provide for and be available to them.

Example 4. If I am *courageous,* then I will follow my heart. And that is important because sometimes I am too scared to do the things that I know, deep inside, are important to me. Being courageous will help me speak my truth and do courageous things — whether or not I have the support of my friends or family.

The merit of these exercises comes from exploring the importance of these values, the meaning they carry, the way in which they guide our behavior and ultimately, how living them brings us meaning and fulfillment.

What Am I Supposed to Be Doing?

Most of us have met people who are clear about their calling or life purpose. These individuals seem to be fully present in their work and life, they enjoy what they do, and they see how their work makes a difference. They know what they are supposed to be doing. Many spiritual traditions teach that all human beings have a Spirit-inspired vocation, not a job or career so much as a life direction or purpose.

I, too, believe that each of us has a deeper purpose, a reason for being on this earth. Often referred to as a calling or mission, our deeper purpose is why we exist. Although it is larger than our work, our work is one avenue we can use to achieve our purpose. For example, Sue's purpose was to facilitate health. In her earlier career, she did so by working in a hospital. As she became clearer that what she was supposed to do was to promote spiritual health, she realized that she was not limited to fulfilling her deeper purpose only through work. She took every opportunity available, inside and outside of work, to foster spiritual growth in others.

Kelly, an organizational management consultant, identified "ministry" as part of her reason for being here. She said her first career as a nurse had a lot of ministry in it. No wonder that historically, nurses were called ministering angels. While ministry is still her reason for being, she is called to "minister" in other venues outside of nursing, including through her personal life.

When we uncover our deeper purpose, we are "called" to fulfill it in every aspect of our lives. The call to fulfill this purpose does not allow us to artificially separate work from the rest of our life. More so, it calls us to live in alignment with our deeper purpose — always.

Although they may not use the terms "purpose, mission or calling," people with spirit at work share clarity about why they are here and what they are supposed to do. The physician's purpose was to release "dis-ease;" the parking attendant, to make others happy; the police officer, to help others; the educator, to facilitate learning and transformation; and the professor, to be a seed planter.

A mission or purpose statement answers the questions: What is my life about? What am I here for? What matters to me? What do I stand for? What moves my heart? What is mine to do and no one else's? Developing a personal mission statement is a way to articulate our life purpose. We can then use it as a guide in making choices, for example about the work we do, how we use our time or how we spend our money. In particular, a mission or purpose statement can help us find meaning in our work by linking what we do with our personal mission.

Again, there are several books devoted to uncovering your purpose or mission statement. For example, Laurie Beth Jones[18] provides exercises to identify what she calls our path. I am interested in providing you with the opportunity to explore what you are "supposed to be doing," then taking it a step further to help you see the relationship between your work and what you are supposed to be doing — to uncover the deeper meaning your work holds for you.

You have already been collecting material that will help determine your purpose.

> ↓ In Chapter Two, you recalled a time when you had spirit at work. That was likely a time when you were living your deeper purpose. Recall that experience again. What was it about that experience that related to your

deeper purpose? What was the connection? What were you doing? Have you had other peak experiences? If so, what were the elements of those experiences? How did these experiences contribute to your deeper purpose?

- ⚜ In Chapter Three, you identified the defining moments in your life. You examined how those significant events or experiences influenced your world view and career choice.

- ⚜ In the previous chapter, you took the time to appreciate yourself and the unique contribution you make through work. You identified what you value most about yourself when you are doing your best and how you make this world a better place through your work. Then you answered the question, "Why does that matter?" The answer is directly related to your deeper purpose — why you are here.

- ⚜ In witnessing your life, you were mindful of what matters to you. You identified the things you love, that give you meaning and the most fulfillment. You collected items that symbolized what fills your heart.

- ⚜ In sorting your values, you determined those values, both terminal and instrumental, that held the most meaning for you. You uncovered your signature value.

- ⚜ Then, in the *If Game*, you declared why they were important to you.

Now you are ready to use this new understanding to put together a purpose statement.

Craft a Purpose Statement

A purpose statement is an excellent tool to help us keep clear about what is important and why we are doing what we are doing. Here is my purpose statement:

My life purpose is to inspire, guide and foster personal growth and the creation of spirit at work so that individuals experience fulfillment and meaning through work.

A leader may have the following as his purpose statement:

> My purpose is to lead, champion and support others to grow personally and professionally so that they can develop their potential and be the best they can be at work and in their private lives.

A purpose statement is composed of four parts:

1. **The how:** the actions you take (e.g., facilitate, sustain, build, collect, lead, promote, heal, serve, teach)

2. **The what:** values, principles, purpose or cause to which you are committed (e.g., peace, conservation, health, communication, spirituality, safety, well-being, education)

3. **For whom or what cause:** the audience or concern (e.g., children, health, environment, wildlife, business)

4. **For what purpose:** outcome

What is your purpose statement? Use the following guide to develop yours.

My life purpose is to [write three verbs here] (1) _____,

(1) _____, and (1) _____

[write what you are committed to here] (2) _____

among/for/on behalf [write your audience or cause or concern here]

(3) _____ so

[write the outcome you wish to see here] (4) _____

_____

_____

Play with the words until it feels right, but don't get caught up in seeking the perfect purpose statement. I find that the energy comes from the recurring themes and the words you use to capture the purpose. Also, don't feel that you need to stay with the above format. Follow your intuition to express yourself in a meaningful way.

Once you have your purpose statement, see if you can find two words that capture its essence. Be sure the first word ends in "-ing" as it denotes action. The second word answers "what?" — what you are trying to achieve. Examples are: inspiring learning, creating energy, generating health, building connections, enriching relationships, promoting peace, stimulating thoughts, sustaining families and exploring possibilities. Write your two words — Dick Richards[19] calls this your *genius* — on an index card or small piece of paper and draw a symbol that reflects the meaning for you. Keep this card in a place where you will see it on a regular basis, for example, on your computer or bathroom mirror or in your agenda. Each time you see it, pause and reflect on why you are here and what you are supposed to be doing. How can you fulfill your purpose and act upon these words through your work?

If after you go through these exercises you still have difficulty identifying your deeper purpose, you may wish to "be" with it for a while. It may be that you are trying too hard. So be with it and see if, in the next while, you start to notice things. Does an idea keep coming back? Do previous experiences keep popping up? Do certain words pop into your mind? Write them down as they come to you. Be mindful not to pass judgment but to accept them as they present themselves. Your inability to uncover your deeper purpose may be because something is holding you back, and this exercise is an excellent way to get past these obstacles. Whether or not you have written a purpose statement, you have engaged in a process of uncovering what is important to you — and that is what matters.

Another way to get to what really matters is to create our own legacy. We all want to leave a legacy — some indication that our life mattered and we made a difference in the world. What are the events in your life: the things you have accomplished, the people you have loved, the things of which you are proudest and the memories you cherish? What is it that you want to be remembered for? Where do you want to leave your mark?

Writing our own legacy is like an out-of-body experience. It helps us see the bigger picture of what is truly important. The exercise gives the opportunity to reflect on how we are living and whether it is in alignment with what we say is important. Unlike when we really die, we have a chance to change how we are doing things and impact our legacy now. A format is provided in the companion guidebook.

Reflection. This exercise has a way of going really deep. When you are finished, arrange to spend some time by yourself, just to be with what came up. Go for a walk, take a bath or meditate — whatever will allow you to synthesize what you have just learned. Then ask yourself, "What is my deeper purpose? What am I here to do? How do I want to live my life?" Then go back and see if you can craft or edit your purpose statement.

Living purposefully and consciously is key to experiencing spirit at work. In order to live with conscious intent, we must know who we are, what is important, what we stand for and our deeper reason for being.

You engaged in a process of reflection and self-examination to determine what gives you personal meaning. You practiced mindfulness. You explored your personal values. You developed a personal mission or purpose statement. I expect you now have greater clarity about your deeper purpose in life. The next step is to determine how to live out your purpose and examine how your work (or the way you work) contributes to that purpose. It begins with being intentional.

Be Intentional

> *Your intention towards somebody is the most important aspect of what you are doing. If your intention is kindness and compassion, you are not there for you; you are there for them. Intention is part of the spirituality about how you go about things. You find you cannot do it any other way, or it will not work for them and it will not work for you. So there is only one way to go about it.*
>
> —Ben, physiotherapist

Intent is the unseen motivation underlying our action. Thus, all actions are congruent with our intent. Being intentional is about living on purpose. It is the difference between having desires and dreams and following them through. Thus, being intentional is the precursor to transforming aspirations into action. Consciously choosing how to achieve these aims is the essence of living with intent.

Living with intent requires identifying concerns or passions worthy of commitment. This process includes questioning the purpose of our work. People with spirit at work are clear that their intent is not about them, but rather about making a contribution towards others and society as a whole. For many, these concerns are linked to their purpose in life. In living with intent, most individuals consciously translate their passion, concerns or mission into personally defined and intrinsically meaningful goals. They then act on personal projects, life tasks and work responsibilities related to these goals.

Intent Underlies All Decisions

Behind every decision and subsequent action lies our intent, even if we are not conscious of it. Yet our behavior doesn't always reveal intent.

For example, several employees in a shared work unit may work extra-long hours. The first is committed to improving customer service and is working to clean up the backlog. The second is seeking a promotion and thus working for personal gain. A third is using work to avoid difficulties with family. The behavior appears the same, but the intent spells important differences.

Whether or not we are aware of our intentions, they determine our actions. So on one level, behavior is aligned with intent. In the above example, the top priority of the employee committed to improving customer service is the customer. This employee is the most likely to have the customer's needs in mind.

Ah, but just because the second employee is working late in hopes of getting a promotion doesn't mean she isn't concerned about customer service, you might point out. And you may be right. However, if a promotion is her priority, what do you think will happen if a conflict between customer service and a promotion opportunity arises? Perhaps the boss asks her to do something that is incongruent with customer service. If she feels her promotion is threatened, which do you think she will choose?

Finally, the third employee's late hours — which he puts in to avoid family issues — do not point to any concern on his part with customer service. Even though he is working extended hours, he may have no interest in customer service.

Beware of making assumptions about intent based on first glances at behavior; similar behavior in no way implies similar intent.

Align Intent and Purpose and the Behavior Will Follow

Our actions are always in sync with our intent. Whether the intent is conscious or unconscious, it just happens. Unfortunately for most of us, intent is generally unconscious unless we make a real effort otherwise. In addition to being mindful of intent, people with spirit at work go a step further and choose to align their intent with their purpose. The appropriate behaviors follow.

Their sequence looks like this:

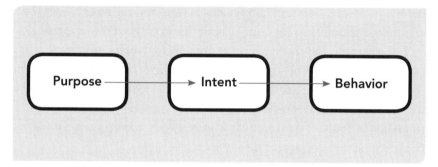

This process became very clear to me during a disagreement I was having with my husband. I don't recall the details of the conversation, but I remember my upset and anger towards him. My instinct was to withdraw and go away. At that moment, I had no desire to continue the conversation or resolve the disagreement. I was that angry. Then, in a flash, I reminded myself that I chose to marry this man with the intent of sharing the rest of my life with him. And my intent was to share a happy life, not be part of a relationship filled with upset. In an instant, something shifted inside of me. I knew that I could no longer hold onto my stance. Although I would need some time to release my upset before I could open up the conversation again, I was able to serve notice that I was interested in working through this issue. When I was ready to begin the conversation again, my intent was different, as was my behavior. I was looking for a win-win, so I became interested not only in getting my story across, but in listening with deeper understanding to my husband's story. I felt a sense of alignment again because my behaviors were congruent with my intent and deeper purpose. Let me be clear that I am not always in this state of enlightenment, but when I get glimpses of it, I know that I am living in alignment.

We are continually faced with choices, yet most of the time we don't recognize that a choice is available. With our fast-paced lives, we find ourselves going from one event or assignment to another without examining whether the matters filling up our days, weeks and years are in alignment with our deeper purpose. Often, it is only when we are faced with despair or a crisis that we begin to question our deeper purpose and examine how our behaviors contribute to that purpose. It does not have to be this way.

Sometimes I think there never seems to be enough time to do everything. Then I hear this inner voice: "Yes, but there is always enough time to do what matters."

So, how are you spending your time? Where do you place your energy? What do you do first? When do you do the important stuff? How do you decide? Do you decide? Start with what matters most. When you do the important stuff first, the rest will follow. And if it doesn't, well, it was not so important.

You need only a jar, small rocks, pebbles and sand to demonstrate this. The jar signifies time, the rocks symbolize what truly matters, the pebbles represent less important things, and the sand is the remaining small stuff. What happens if we fill up the jar with sand first? There is no room for the rocks or the pebbles, right? It is full. But if we start with the rocks (do first things first), there is still lots of room for the pebbles and sand.

This is like life. If we start with what's really important to us, we feel energized and more able and willing to do less important things required of us. Have you ever noticed when you take time out of your busy schedule to do something important — like spend time with a troubled colleague, help a parent in need or play ball with your child — you still seem to get the everyday stuff done? Even if the lawn mowing had to wait for a few days or you had grilled cheese for dinner, so what? What matters is that you chose to spend your time in a way that was meaningful.

This is often what happens at work as well. How many of us try to take care of the less important items before we tackle the big assignment? We answer phone calls, respond to emails and meet with colleagues to free up time to do this important work. Have you noticed that the emails and memos never stop coming, and that really, we are never free? There always seems to be something to do before we can get to that important project. That's the sand — it just keeps on coming. We use our best energy, the time we are fresh and clear-thinking, to do the mundane part of our job. Then we use what is left — both time and energy — to be creative. When we live with intent, we begin with what is important. We begin with the rocks. The rest will follow.

Invitation. Choose a clear glass container or vase. Collect enough rocks to fill the container two-thirds full. Be particular about choosing the rocks as they represent what really matters to you. If you like, label the rocks. Fill your container, leaving room at the top for other really important things that might come forward. Put your collection in a prominent place as a reminder to do first things first. Know that there will always be room for the pebbles and sand.

When we shift our intent, we shift our priorities and surprisingly, we often become uncomfortable. Not only do people around us resist this change, but we are faced with many challenges. Some of us want to do it all. We want to be the best spouse, the greatest parent, the top employee, a faithful friend, and so on. There's a saying that goes, "You can do anything you want; you just can't do it all." We must be selective in how we choose to spend our time and live our lives, and the best way I know of doing this is to align intent with purpose.

Alignment Check

Drawing from your previous work (particularly your purpose statement) or your inner wisdom, think about what is most important in your life. Now consider what is occupying your time. What is the relationship between what you say is important and how you spend your time? Are you living in alignment?

You might find yourself saying, "Yes, but I have to do the shopping and the laundry and the. . ." and to some extent, that is true. Maybe the question is: How much of it do you have to do? When is it good enough? Because if it is also true that you want to do what is important to you, then something has to give, and hopefully it is the things of lesser importance. Today spend some time doing what matters to you, and less time on what does not. Then in a moment of quiet time, reflect back on how that felt. See if you can do it again tomorrow.

We have a saying in our home that we clean the house for company. While I appreciate having a clean house, that is one area I have decided to let go so that I can use my time doing more important things, such as building relationships. So, when we invite friends or family over, we are thrilled to have the company and a clean house. Now *that* is a real bonus!

Alignment Check at Work

I would like you to repeat this process and complete an alignment check at work. What are the ten most important things you do at work? How do you spend your time? What is the relationship between what you say is important at work and how you spend your time? Is there anything that you would like to be doing differently to live in alignment with what you say is important at work?

> Neal was a very effective car salesman who had been promoted to a management role. Although he appreciated the recognition the promotion gave him, he found something very dissatisfying about his new work. When he had completed the above spirit-at-work exercise, Neal realized he was out of alignment.
>
> What he appreciated most about his work was the opportunity to work directly with customers and help them make effective choices. His new administrative role limited his contact with his beloved customers. Once he realized that, Neal negotiated an arrangement that allowed him to do sales one day a week. That was enough to keep him happy and he felt like he was a better manager as a result.

Focus Your Work on the Higher Good

People with spirit at work are clear that their intent is not about them personally, but rather about making a contribution towards others and society as a whole. They see their work as service for the higher good. The real estate agent was not selling houses, but helping clients find a home and community. The hairdresser was not cutting hair, but helping her clients feel and look good. The parking attendant was not parking cars, but making people happy. The physician was not prescribing medicine, but releasing "dis-ease." The organizational consultant was not providing advice, but helping others be the best they could be. What is it that you do? What is the higher good of your work?

We feel most purposeful when we are working towards a higher good. And we are most fulfilled when we are on purpose. That is why people who live their mission or deeper purpose tend to be the most fulfilled. Every job or career involves an aspect of higher good — some are just more obvious. Sometimes I find that this simply involves understanding the deeper meaning in our particular work (or the work of the organization) and appreciating our contribution. This is often the case with administrative support employees or custodial staff. They generally do not see how their work links with the higher purpose of the organization. For example, the janitor in a school might have difficulty seeing how his work contributes to the education of students. But can you imagine what our schools would be like without janitors? They indeed are very important players in a child's education. They are part of the team that creates learning experiences for children.

In other situations, we require a shift in our attitude. As a society, we have been conditioned to think about ourselves and about getting ahead. We have been trained in a win-lose way of thinking. The thought of serving a higher good and seeing our work as an act of service is incongruent with this mindset. Deeper fulfillment comes from doing for others.

Moreover, focusing your intent on the higher good of others or a cause must be done from the heart and without attachments or expectation for reward. The deeper purpose must be the act of service and not the expectation. The martyr who does everything for everyone else because she feels she has to is not serving others from the heart. Similarly, the person who does for others out of guilt will not experience spirit at work. The employee who agrees to a project only because he wants to get ahead will not experience fulfilling work. The person who accepts a position out of greed will eliminate her chances of job satisfaction. It comes back to our intent. For spirit at work to occur, our intent must be to serve the higher good.

Spirit at work comes from aligning your actions with your intent and deeper purpose. The intent must be for higher good — that is, the betterment of others or a cause. An intent for personal gain negates the chance of spirit at work, which is why so many people are without spirit at work. They have lost touch with what drew them to their profession in the first place. This is not to say that we should not want to get ahead. It is just that if getting ahead is our primary reason for doing what we are doing, we are not truly serving others. We are serving ourselves. Serving ourselves coincides with lower levels of fulfillment, whereas serving others correlates with a higher level of fulfillment.[20] Interestingly though, people find that living a life of purpose and living with intent results in great personal gain and fulfillment. The gift of giving brings with it many personal rewards. More about this in the following chapter.

Working with Intent at Work

Our thoughts and intent focus the flow of our energy. Therefore it is essential that we have clarity about both. With this clarity, we can direct our intent and attention to serving others and the higher good. Keep in mind that the matters to which we give our attention grow stronger.

- What is the deeper purpose of your organization's work?
- What is the higher good of your work?
- Whom does your organization serve?
- How does it serve?
- How does your particular work contribute to the organization's deeper purpose and higher good?
- How does the way you do your work contribute to this purpose?
- What is your intent as you do your work?
- Does your intent assist or impede the higher good?
- What gets your attention at work?
- Is this in alignment with your company's deeper purpose?

- How aligned is your intent and attention with the organization's deeper purpose and work towards the higher good?
- What one thing can you do to bring them more into alignment?
- How do your answers fit with your own deeper purpose?

You may find that your answers are very similar to the purpose statement you created in the previous section. If so, you are in a very fortunate position to be living your deeper purpose or passion through your daily work. If not, you have just uncovered the deeper meaning of your particular work and your intent to serve others through this work. Either way, you are on the path to spirit at work.

Integrate Self

I live my faith so that the way I treat people during the day is a reflection of my beliefs.

—Noreen, educator

People with spirit at work strive for integration in all parts of their lives, including within themselves. In doing so, they endeavor to live in alignment with what matters, and they work at being authentic — that is, being who they really are all the time. The goal is to live a life where everything is integrated as opposed to the one most of us are used to, where everything is separate and fragmented. Choosing to live authentically in all dimensions of our life, including work, is essential to the integration of self. Being authentic means being the real you. Being honest. Being true to yourself and your values. Standing up for your beliefs. Expressing yourself fully, even if your views are different from everyone else's views.

A Far Side comic shows a gathering of penguins, one of whom stands in the middle with a big sign that says, "I've got to be me." Can you relate to that penguin? How authentic are you? Do you have a public and a private face? By this I mean are you different at work than at home or with your friends? Would your family be surprised to hear stories about how you are at work or vice versa?

As a young adult, I came face-to-face with this experience. A friend and I decided to host a sleigh ride. We created a guest list that included friends, family, work colleagues and neighbors. In my excitement, I skipped over the fact that none of these people had ever met. It was a time I was living a fragmented life; I kept my work, social and family life separate. The parts of myself that I shared, and even the conversations I had with each group, were different. When I realized the little glitch, I panicked. When that didn't help, I comforted myself with the thought that people wouldn't show up. Wrong! In looking back, I think those who attended were very interested in meeting people in my "other" life, and were curious about why I had previously exhibited such a strong need to keep them apart. I thought of every excuse I could to cancel the event, but my friend wouldn't hear of it. As it turned out, I was the only one who was nervous and worried. Everyone had a great time and, for the first time, they had an opportunity to learn about the many faces of Val. That event was a defining moment in my life — a time when I decided to be more authentic, to be who I was in all aspects of my life.

Living authentically refers to the ability to express our complete self — physical, emotional, intellectual and spiritual — all the time, including at work. This expression of one's complete self at work is often referred to as "bringing your whole self to work." As one person said, "I am all of who I am at work, but work is not all of me. I am much more than that." This person knew she was more than her work, but when she was at work, she was her complete self. If you truly wanted to be all of who you are at work, what would need to change?

Being integrated involves functioning in tandem with our inner nature — that is, our values, beliefs and interests. For those of us who have spirit at work, this sense of alignment, or match, extends to work. In particular, we experience alignment between personal goals and actions and our deeper life purpose.

When we are integrated, we see how everything we do, including our work, is related to our deeper purpose. Everything is connected. It is not fixed. There is give and take. We accommodate. We integrate. So when we are called at work by the daycare to pick up a sick child, we pause our work and pick up our child or make alternative plans without guilt. We are clear that caring for our child is part of our deeper purpose. Similarly, when we need to bring some work home or stay late to finish a project, we expect to do so, because that too is part of our purpose. When we are integrated, there is an ebb and flow so that all priorities are accommodated. This is important because there needs to be room for all our priorities. If we focus all our energy and attention on one priority, we begin to cut ourselves off from the things that matter to us and we begin to lead a fragmented life.

This is not to say that we give equal attention to all priorities in our life all the time. That is the concern I have with the notion of living a balanced life. It assumes that everything is equal. When I think about balance, I think about trying to balance a teeter-totter. It is very difficult to get the exact balance where both sides of the teeter-totter are at the same height from the ground. One side is always higher than the other. And the energy expended in trying to make them equal can be enormous. Not to mention the frustration that goes along with "not being in balance" or the guilt about "not living a balanced life." Not everything is in balance. Not all priorities carry equal weight. There are times in our life when we are called to give more attention to particular areas, be that raising children, helping elderly parents, developing our career, pursuing secondary education, living our passion or regaining health.

Practicing integration is different than striving for balance. People view family, work and personal interests, for example, as part of a larger and connected whole, rather than as separate and competing parts. Moreover, each of these life tasks provides an opportunity to fulfill our deeper purpose. Rather than attempting to maintain an equal balance, we need to give varying emphasis to each responsibility as need and priority dictates over time.

Is your life fragmented or integrated? Is your work and the rest of your life separated or connected? If you drew your "pie of life" — in which each slice represented the important aspects in your life (e.g., family, health, work, hobbies, finances, spirituality) — what would it look like? How satisfied are you with the size of the varying pieces? Is there anything you would like to change? Any area to which you'd like to redirect your energy? Give yourself permission to let go of the need for a balanced life and live your life in line with what you have identified as your priorities. Honor what you know is important to you.

The Match Between Our Goals and Our Deeper Purpose

Previously, you clarified the values that hold the greatest meaning for you and crafted a purpose statement. You identified what is most important to you and weighed those things against how you spend your time and you discovered how you can live with intent by serving the higher good. In the last exercise, you allotted a proportion to what's most important and considered how each aspect of your life contributes to your purpose. Given that wealth of information, what would you say your three most important goals are right now at this stage of your life?

What are the three most important goals at work? How do these goals fit with your deeper purpose? How do they fit with each other? How can you more fully integrate these goals into your life? What has to go? What has to give? How can you bring these goals into your life without ignoring the other things in your life that matter? What is one thing you can do to give life to each of these goals?

The Power of Positive Thought

We create our own luck through our attitude and how we see the world.

—Karla, landscape designer

To live purposefully and consciously is to be aware of the power of thought and how our thoughts affect our lives. We have a choice about our thoughts. Louise Hay[21] in *The Power Is Within You* taught us that they are just thoughts and thoughts can be changed. For example, we can choose positive thoughts, decide against certain thoughts and redirect negative thoughts. When we select our thoughts; we can choose to see the best in each situation even in less than desirable circumstances.

Wayne Dyer convinced us that "When you change the way you look at things, the things you look at change." By reframing students' issues as a challenge, Sheila, the graduate coordinator, changed the way she looked at things:

I'm the type of person who cares about people and is interested in what makes them tick. Otherwise, I would probably see issues that students bring to me as problems — as real frustrating, unpleasant problems that I have to deal with. But I no longer see them that way. I see them as challenges and I think, "Here's a way I can help somebody. This person needs help. Now what can I do for him?"

Sheila's "what makes them tick" approach influences how she interacts with students. Her thoughts about work definitely impact how she works. Because she sees her work as an act of service, she welcomes the opportunity to help others.

Others choose to "see the poetry in the everyday," which translates into seeking and finding the beauty that is present despite existing conditions. The more we look for the beauty, the more we see it. Our attitudes and world view affect our thoughts, which influence how we see and experience the world. If we believe that the world is friendly, we see a friendly world and thus act differently than if we saw the world as hostile. Albert Einstein said, "The most important decision we ever make is whether we believe that we live in a friendly universe or a hostile one." Being selective in our thoughts and reactions is an important factor in making positive choices.

Our Mind Cannot Tell the Difference Between a Thought and the Real Thing

Read the following instructions before you close your eyes and complete the visualization.

> Think about a juicy lemon. In your mind observe the color, feel the texture of the skin and temperature, and smell the scent. Now see yourself slicing the lemon in half. As you slice, the lemon juice begins to drip. Maybe some even gets on your hands. Now open your mouth and bite into the lemon. Once you get a taste, open your eyes and come back.

What was that experience like for you? Were you able to use your senses to recreate a lemon? What was it like to think of biting into the lemon? Most people in my workshops say they feel the saliva increase in their mouth and they shudder or grimace when they bite into the lemon. Some pull back and make a sound.

This is a very simple example of how powerful our thoughts are. It also confirms research that the brain does not know the difference between a real act and an imagined act. Your body reacted as if you really bit into the lemon — except you didn't. Thoughts, negative or positive, have the same effect on our body and emotions as true-life sensations.

I am married to a wonderful man, but our concept of time couldn't be more different. When Fred says he will be there at 5:00, he means 5ish. That might be 5:00, 5:15 or 5:30. In contrast, I tend to be "right on time." So if I say I will be there at 5:00, I will likely be there at 4:59 so as not to waste any time. You can imagine our first years of marriage.

When our son was born a few years after we were married, I took a year off work to be at home with him. Joey had colic, so I looked forward to Fred's arrival home from work. One evening, Fred said that he would be home by 5:00. I knew that Fred was an "ish" person, so when he didn't show up at 5:00, I thought he was held up at the office and would be home by 5:30. When he didn't show up by 5:30, I told myself he'd been caught in traffic. When he didn't show up by 6:00, I convinced myself that he'd been in an accident. And when he didn't show up by 6:15, I was planning my life as a single parent. I laugh as I recall this story, but it was not funny at the time. And less funny was the fact that my body reacted as if all this had really happened. My heart rate increased, my blood pressure went up and I started to sweat. My body did not know I had created this experience in my mind. Even when Fred arrived, fully alive and intact, I was unable to release the feelings inside.

Long since, of course, we've worked out this discrepancy. When Fred learned how important time was to me, he made great efforts to be on time, and when he was going to be late, he would phone me. I, on the other hand, decided to be less dramatic and to remind myself that Fred loses track of time. It works beautifully.

• • • • • • •

There is never a moment when people are not thinking — and their thoughts are either positive or negative. Unfortunately, we tend to have more negative than positive thoughts. In fact, we have up to 65,000 thoughts a day and sixty-five percent of them are negative. Negative thoughts can eat at our confidence, our self-esteem and our spirit.

They can prevent us from doing what we really want to do. Moreover, "negative self-talk" impacts our immune system. It takes a great toll on our bodies and sense of well-being.

On the other hand, the power of *positive thoughts* to affect our experience of life has long been recognized, embraced and promoted as a path to wellness. Several books have been written on the effect of positive thinking. Norman Vincent Peale is one of the best known for his book *The Power of Positive Thinking.*[22]

More recently, scientists are proving that the power of positive thought impacts our health, well-being and motivation. A study at Northern Arizona University showed that a group of runners was able to achieve an overall twelve percent increase in the test group's strength just by thinking and speaking positively about their muscle systems.

In another study about visualization in the mid-1990s, Stanford University took two groups of basketball players through an experiment. One group practiced shooting baskets. The second group didn't step into the gym; instead, they only visualized taking shots. Amazingly, the group that used visualization improved their shooting skills by thirty percent over the group that physically practiced shooting hoops with a basketball. Both of these studies demonstrate the power of the mind-body connection.

This discovery is not limited to sports. Many successful business people credit their success to their positive thoughts. When we think positively and visualize a positive future, we tend to have positive experiences.

Visualize Your Heart's Desire

Practicing visualization is a very simple yet effective way to achieve our goals. Use this visualization regularly, even daily, to prepare yourself for attaining your aspiration.

1. Find yourself a quiet place where you will be uninterrupted.

2. Quiet the mind by taking a few cleansing breaths and then observe your breath until you feel yourself slow down and relax. (You may wish to begin with the basic meditation outlined in Chapter Eight.)

3. When you feel ready, visualize the goal you are trying to accomplish. Perhaps it is a new job, having a successful conversation with a difficult employee, or a raise.
   a. Let go of any limiting thinking.
   b. See yourself achieving your goal.
   c. Observe the conversations, body language and interactions.
   d. Feel the support of others.
   e. Notice that all the conditions necessary to achieve your goal are present.
4. Feel the emotions of achieving your desires. Hold onto this emotion as you prepare to return from the visualization.

Our thoughts are very powerful. They are the inner conversations that we continue to have with ourselves. People who begin to consciously modify these inner conversations and assumptions to reflect positive thoughts report an almost immediate improvement in their performance. Their energy increases and things seem to go better.

If positive thoughts are so powerful, why do we hold onto so many negative thoughts? Negative thoughts are attitudes — "It won't work," "I'm not good enough," "Nothing comes my way," "We never get anything." These attitudes, built from the feedback of parents, friends, society and self, are habits. And they quickly form our self-image and our world view. We maintain these attitudes by the inner conversations we constantly have with ourselves, both consciously and subconsciously. To move to positive thoughts, we require a change of attitude.

A Change of Attitude

The first step in changing our attitudes is to change our inner conversations. What conversations are you having with yourself? What messages have you accepted to be true?

Stream-of-consciousness writing can help to identify the many attitudes we hold. It is a powerful way of writing because it taps into our unconscious and often supplies us with information not readily available. At the top of a blank page (or in the guidebook), write the question "What attitudes direct my life?" Then just start writing the first thought that comes to mind. Do not judge or alter any thoughts. Just write. And keep writing without trying to analyze what you are putting down. Write until you feel you are done, but stay with it for at least ten minutes. The longer you keep writing, the more your unconscious will release these attitudes to you and the more surprised you will be.

If you encounter difficulty in getting started, think about the sayings you grew up with, for example:

- Everything is possible.
- It is a dog-eat-dog world.
- There is enough for everyone.
- I work to live, not live to work.
- It is not what you know but who you know.
- If you can dream it, you can build it.

You may also use the following prompts:

- I believe (that)...
- If only...
- It is just my luck...
- I always...
- I never...

Once you are finished, underline the positive attitudes and circle the negative ones. How do they compare? What attitudes are about work? What attitudes influence how you do your work? What is the source of these attitudes? Did they come from your parents, friends, church, society or personal experiences? Which of these attitudes impede your spirit at work and which contribute to it? Which continue to serve you well and which are no longer needed and can be released? Given where you are today, are there any new attitudes you wish to adopt?

We are free to choose our attitudes. Viktor Frankl, an Austrian psychiatrist, was captured by the Nazis during World War II and held prisoner at the Auschwitz concentration camp. His wife and parents were murdered by the Schutzstaffel, a major Nazi organization under Adolf Hitler. It was a devastating time for him and others. Frankl described how this organization controlled every part of his life, including whether he lived or died. But he discovered that the one thing they could not control was his attitude. In his book *Man's Search for Meaning: An Introduction to Logotherapy*,[23] Frankl states:

> Man is not free from conditions. But he is free to take a stand in regard to them. He decides whether he will face up or give in. Whether or not he will let himself be determined by his conditions.

> Everything can be taken from a man but the last of any human freedoms — to choose one's attitude in any given set of circumstances, to choose one's way.

By choosing our thoughts, we choose our way. By changing our thoughts and our attitudes, we change our reality.

Choose Consciously

I feel an awakening to the fact that we can either choose to be a part of the building process or we can do things, make decisions and think in ways that actually, somehow, abridge that process.

—Rowena, professor

Choice is the power to make decisions. A conscious choice provides each of us with an element of control over what happens in our life. Whether those choices are conscious or unconscious, they carry responsibility. Zukav[24] calls unconscious choices such as anger, jealously or fear a *reaction* and conscious choices a *response*. Unlike an immediate reaction, when we make a conscious choice, we are able to step back and choose an action. That action will create consequences for which we are willing to take responsibility.

Even if they are angry, people who strive to make conscious choices are aware that they choose their thoughts and subsequent action, and that this action will result in certain consequences. Sometimes only a moment is available to choose between a reaction and a response. As we practice conscious intent, the moment gets longer.

Each choice brings a possible future into reality. There are many forks in the road. If we choose consciously rather than react, we are in a position to consider the consequences of our choices and whether those results are consistent with our intent. If the result is not what we expect or desire, we can examine our intent and choose an alternative action. If we are not getting the results we hoped for, it is time to take a second look at our intent — because behavior is always aligned with intent. Perhaps we are not clear about our intent, or maybe we have a shadow intent that is stronger than our initial intent. Either way, it is a clear indication that it is time to re-examine our intent.

Each of us has made many choices over the course of our life — to get married, start a family, purchase a home or vehicle, accept or quit a job, or move to another city. These generally involve a lot of thought and commitment. The consequences are great. Yet how many of us assessed these decisions against our intent or deeper purpose? How many of us considered the consequences of those decisions? Really, how many of those decisions were conscious?

When I ask people how they came to their job, many say they needed a job and it was available. They applied and got it. Some, like Ken or Rose, are able to find deeper meaning in their work and learn to love it. Many others are unsatisfied and unfulfilled. They did not make conscious choices and as a result, are living with the consequences.

In fact, some may have chosen not to make a choice. Have you ever done that? Decided not to decide? The funny thing is, choosing not to make a decision is still a decision. It is impossible to stop making choices or decisions. Here is an example.

For years, my family talked about taking a trip to Europe. We planned for it several times. We took books out from the library, bought maps and spent time with a travel agent. We saved money for the trip. Yet we did not book the flight. We didn't make a decision not to go; we just did not make the arrangements. For some unconscious reason, we chose not to go on this trip — at least, not then.

Conscious choices stem from having conscious intent, which paves the road to spirit at work. As we assume responsibility for our experiences and the results we want to see, our lives become more meaningful. Conscious intent is the power to make a difference.

The Moment of Choice

Think of the times over the last week when you made conscious choices. Perhaps it was to close a journal and play with your child, go for a walk, take your spouse out on a date, call a friend or simply be kind. What conscious choices have you made at work? Maybe you expressed thanks, helped out a colleague, stayed late and finished a project, complimented a customer or appreciated your own contribution. What did it feel like to be conscious?

Think of some examples over the last week when you reacted rather than responded. Can you find examples both at work and outside work? What was different between choosing consciously and reacting? Which one felt more comfortable? Which action brought the preferred results? If you could do it all over again, what if anything would you change?

Go back to the times your decision was conscious. Can you find the *moment of choice* — the moment that was available to choose between a reaction and a response? What about the times you reacted? Can you see where the moment of choice was? How long did you have it? How will you be able to recognize it in the future?

Over the next while, try to be mindful of the moment of choice. As it presents itself, see if you can pause and choose your response. Don't worry if you miss it. Sometimes it is just a flash, but as you continue to look for it, it will become more obvious. In the beginning, you may notice it but not be able to pull together a conscious response. That is alright, too. Your awareness is increasing. Be gentle with yourself and use the experience to grow.

Engage in Transformative Action

> *Transformative action is the difference between going about your day in kind of a fog and routine and applying yourself and your passion to make a difference.*
>
> —Noreen, educator

Living consciously and purposefully requires that we take action. Gary Zukav in *The Seat of the Soul*[25] says, "Intention is the difference between having a vision and bringing it into the world. Inspiration is common, but inspired action is rare." Knowing our life purpose, being intentional, living an integrated life, selecting positive thoughts and making conscious choices are very important, but they are not enough if you want to have spirit at work.

To cultivate spirit at work, we must engage in inspired and transformative action. It is not enough just to do something; our work must make a difference, a contribution, to others. And we must appreciate the contribution we are making.

Intent is the motivation behind transformative action. It is what transforms a desire, goal or mission into initiatives and accomplishments. Those who engage in transformative action tend to be proactive and demonstrate a "take charge" attitude and "just do it" behavior. If something needs to be done, they don't look around to see who else can do it. Nor do they check to see if it is in their job description. If they see a need, they just do it. For example, Lana, a resident care worker, takes the advocacy part of her job very seriously. She speaks for those who cannot speak for themselves, even if it gets her in trouble. The real estate agent's intent was to facilitate successful moves for her clients, so she developed connections with other realtors in other cities and was able to refer her clients, thus helping with the transition to the new city. The police officer developed relationships with members in the community in order to have the necessary resources to help others. This ability to develop and access resources is a common occurrence among people with spirit at work. They are clear about their intent and do what they need to do to fulfill it.

The people I interviewed exemplified openness to new ideas, experiences and outcomes. For some, this meant surrendering control and letting go. For others, it was finding courage to pursue important matters or interests, including a new job or career. When it became clear that Noreen did not have spirit at work, even though she loved her work as a teacher, she made the decision to change careers. When Karla recognized that it was time to work in another area, she gave herself a year to come up with a plan for another career. Becoming a landscape designer required that she go back to school for two years.

When we have spirit at work, we take responsibility for our careers. We pursue ongoing training, skill development and job experience, which in turn foster fulfillment of goals or intent. The physician knew how important her training was, so she kept abreast of current research. Similarly, the physiotherapist believed that his training provided him with the basis to complete his intent, so he welcomed the opportunity to learn more. When we take responsibility for our work experience, we don't wait for our employer to send us on a course or fund our training. We see the connection between ongoing learning and professional development and seek it out. People with spirit at work do not worry about competency requirements, because they have far surpassed the expectations.

While transformative action is about action, it is about taking the right action — action that really means something. Most of us lead full lives, but the question is, what are we doing? Really, what is it that we are doing that makes a difference? Of all that you are doing, what will make you proudest as you near the end of your life? Which will have helped someone or something? We all can be busy doing things, but the key is to choose actions that will make a contribution.

What Are You Saying Yes To?

Earlier, I suggested that not making a decision is making a decision, even if the decision is to not decide immediately. Similarly, by saying yes to one thing, we are deciding to say no to another. In essence, we are making two decisions. When we are not making decisions consciously, it's possible for us to agree to something without considering its consequences. So when you are tempted to say yes, be sure to check what you are saying no to. Strive to say yes to action that will be transformative. Make your effort count.

Too often we wait for all the information or for certainty before we take action. We are scared we might make the wrong decision, so we make no decision. But is making no decision the right decision? Is it any better to make no decision than to make a decision that has potential to contribute to the higher good? People with spirit at work talk about taking bold action. In the same way, Peter Block,[26] consultant and author pushes us to "say yes to uncertainty." Saying yes to uncertainty or being bold doesn't mean we agree to do everything that comes along. Nor does it mean we make impulsive decisions. We use discernment to choose actions that are in line with our deeper purpose and have the potential for transformation. We draw on our intuition and guidance, that inner knowing part of ourselves, to make the best decision. The next step is to be bold and act.

Be Bolder

Paul's story is one of saying yes to uncertainty and being bolder.

> Paul was born with a permanent life-threatening illness. He struggled each day trying to live his life normally while coping with the challenges brought on by his disease.
>
> The public school system wouldn't accept him in regular school because of his health. After eight years of home schooling, Paul dropped out. Later, as an adult, he upgraded and trained to be an accountant.
>
> Upon graduation, he was hired by the federal tax department. He was good at his work, earned the respect of his superiors and colleagues, and made a reasonable wage with good benefits. As the sole provider for his family of four, benefits were important — for both today and tomorrow — given his uncertain health. His friends were relieved knowing that Paul was well situated, with good job security and benefits.
>
> Yet Paul didn't settle into his job. If there was a single characteristic that defined Paul, it was that he had always had the desire to shape his life on his own terms rather than be dictated to by fear and the overwhelming need for security. He had a strong independent spirit and a great belief in his ability to create his future.
>
> So after many discussions with his wife, Paul made the decision to be bold; he handed in his resignation and started his own business. Twenty-five years later, he knows that it was the right decision. Not that it was without struggle, but with hard work, courage and a touch of stubbornness, he has achieved the success and the freedom he always dreamed of.

When was the last time you took bold action at work? Stood up for something that you believed in? Said yes to uncertainty even though you didn't have all the information or resources?

• • • • • • •

Understanding our purpose or having positive intent does not mean we will get up every day and fulfill our purpose. Nor does it mean that every action we take will be transformative. The idea is to be conscious of our purpose and intent and live it as much as we can. The more we are able to live it, the more fulfillment we will bring into our lives.

The practice of *conscious intent* is a new standard for living where we each take responsibility and action for creating the kind of life experience we desire. Rather than going through life on autopilot, we can consciously choose to live with intent. Conscious intent is a critical factor in the development of spirit at work because it reflects our thoughts, values, feelings, actions and goals. Every action is a reflection of intent, whether it is conscious or unconscious.

We can change our consciousness; therefore we can change our conscious thought. For example, if I choose to express compassion instead of frustration or anger with my clients, I have changed my conscious thought. Moreover, I can create my reality with my intent. If I see my life as meaningful, my life has meaning. By choosing to serve the higher good, I create a reality of contributing to society. Changing my thoughts changes my experience. If I find meaning in the work I am doing, my work will become more meaningful. If my work is more meaningful, it becomes more fulfilling and satisfying and I become more committed. Conscious intent and transformative action is at the heart of spirit at work and is a practice we can learn.

Ten Steps to Living Purposefully and Consciously

1. Be mindful: Pause and pay attention.
2. Know what matters: Find your passion.
3. Seek alignment: Ensure a match between what matters and what you do.
4. See your work for the higher good.
5. Be authentic: Bring your whole self to work.
6. Be intentional: Live on purpose.
7. Choose positive thoughts.
8. Make conscious choices.
9. Engage in transformative action.
10. Be ten times bolder.

1. How are you living with purpose?

2. How does work contribute to your life purpose?

3. How does your world view impact how you work?

4. What are the most important values you hold? Is your behavior in alignment with these values?

5. What is it about your work that matters?

6. What is your intent at work?

7. What gets your attention at work?

8. What are you saying yes to?

9. How can you be more integrated, especially at work?

10. What would you do if you were ten times bolder?

11. What one thing might you do differently? What would it take? (Record on page 197)

chapter seven

Cultivate a Spiritual, Values-Based Life

What does it mean to live a spiritual, values-based life? Really, everything I talk about in this book is about living spiritually. The more specific answer to what it means to live a spiritual, values-based life is personal. When I talk about living spiritually I mean being connected to something larger than self, whether that is nature, the transcendent (again, a personal definition) or humanity. To live spiritually also means to be engaged in a continual search for meaning and purpose. It is about living our deeply held values and beliefs, knowing that they shape our behavior. It is about the appreciation of beauty and excellence, which may be accompanied by awe and wonder. Living a spiritual, values-based life is about being optimistic, hopeful and grateful. It is about having spirit and passion.

In the previous chapter, I talked about the connection between experiencing spirit at work and living with deeper meaning and purpose. In your quest for deeper meaning, you got in touch with what matters, sorted through your values and crafted your personal purpose statement. Then you learned how to use intent to live out your deeper purpose. All of these discussions and exercises were designed to assist you to get in touch with your deeper, spiritual self.

The conversation continues in this chapter with a focus on cultivating a spiritual, values-based life by appreciating beauty and excellence, practicing positive virtues, reaching beyond ourselves and connecting with our source of guidance.

Appreciate the Beauty and Excellence that Surrounds You

See the Poetry in the Everyday

Richard Lewis[27] suggests that much of what passes for "ordinary life" is not ordinary at all, but full of potential for spiritual learning. Our ordinary routine contains numerous treasures. The details of our workday — morning commute, coffee break, afternoon meetings, assignments, interaction with others, evening ride home, conversations at the dinner table — contain any number of gifts for our spirit, if only we would allow ourselves to receive them. Lewis calls this "profound ordinariness," which simply means seeing each detail of our everyday life as a gift — truly living one day at a time, one moment at a time.

I first learned about this notion from Karla, the landscape designer with spirit at work. She described it as "seeing the poetry in the everyday."

When we become a witness to our life and all that surrounds us, we begin to notice the wonder and awe that is ever present. We marvel in how the sun comes up and goes down each day. We take delight at seeing a rainbow or falling star. We feel the calm presence of a pet. We share the wonder of play with a child. We taste our favorite foods as if we have never tasted before. We feel comfort in a conversation with a dear friend. We glow in the love of another. That is the poetry in the everyday.

I always knew about the beauty of a sunset and the joy of friendship. But the day I really learned about becoming more aware of the poetry was a day I went to meet my son at the bus.

Joey was in grade one and still too young to walk to and from the school bus. I was working from home, so I was able to do bus drop-off and pick-up. Not wanting to be late (or waste any time waiting), I would watch the clock so that I could be at the bus stop a few moments before the bus arrived. At the appropriate time, I would race up the stairs, slip into my shoes and tear down the street. Because I was in full tilt, it was a challenge to shift from "work" to "mom" mode. And for elementary school children, every day is a big day so they have lots to share, and a need to share it immediately. Joey was no different. Each day he had a story waiting to be told.

Although I listened to Joey and his stories, I was not always fully present. This particular day, however, I thrilled to the feel of his little hand in mine, his excitement and our profound connection. I felt that I was the luckiest person in the world. The experience changed me. From then on, I spent the walk to the bus anticipating the delight of the day.

Where Is the Poetry in Your Day? What would it take for you to see the poetry in the everyday? To appreciate the beauty and excellence that surrounds you? Here are some places to look:

- beauty in nature
- talent in all aspects of life
- compassion for another
- meaningful discussions
- excellence in workmanship
- highly developed musical skills
- sports abilities
- artistic beauty
- acts of kindness or other virtuous behaviors
- the written word
- children at play
- caring and loving relationships.

Find the Meaning in the Meaningless

The title of this section should be "find the meaning in the *seemingly* meaningless" because although it seems like some things hold no meaning, everything has the potential for meaning. I started this book with a story about Ken, the parking lot attendant. At first glance, there is little meaning in being a parking lot attendant. On the surface, all Ken does is sit in a booth and take people's money. Where is the meaning in that? Yet Ken took a "menial" job and turned it into something with great meaning. He was able to find meaning in the seemingly meaningless. Through his work as a parking lot attendant, Ken was able to bring happiness — his deeper purpose — to many throughout his day. His workplace became his venue.

Over the course of my work, I have met numerous taxi drivers. As my family knows (they acquire a "here she goes" look), it doesn't take long for me to pop the question, "And what is it about driving taxi that you enjoy?" I've very quickly learned that taxi drivers are some of the most educated people in the workforce. Many have immigrated to this country with career hopes and dreams, only to find that their education did not meet this country's standards or is not conducive to employment. Their pride and a need to put a roof over their head forced them to take a job driving taxi. Accountants, people with PhDs and engineers are amongst those who drive cab. Some even enjoy it.

Here's Hashim's story.

> At first, he felt ashamed because he was a professional doing meaningless work. But as he started to reflect on what he did, he realized he was able to make a difference in the life of each person who rode in the back seat of his cab. Hashim was there to serve. He ensured that his cab was always clean. He had the daily newspaper available for customers who wanted to keep abreast of current events. He provided a jar of mints and posted reminders to help customers remember personal belongings.
>
> Hashim greeted everyone with a smile and a welcome, then waited for the customer to take the conversational lead. If they wanted to talk, he listened. If they wanted to work, he turned off the radio. If they had an important meeting to get to or an airplane to catch, he did his best to get them there safely and on time. His reputation grew in corporate and political circles. What started as seemingly meaningless work became rewarding and fulfilling. Now Hashim would not think about taking another job.

Meaning can be discovered everywhere, even in senseless or painful experiences. For example, Mothers Against Drunk Drivers (MADD) is an organization that allows parents who've suffered a child's death or injury by a drunk driver to create meaning out of such a senseless event.

But we don't have to wait for disaster to discover meaning. We can begin to uncover it in our day-to-day activities. Grocery shopping can become an opportunity to select and purchase healthy foods to feed your family. Washing dishes or vacuuming can be a time to be in a meditative state. Gardening can be a time to connect with nature and be mindful of the beauty that surrounds you.

What about at work? A waitress may see her work as bringing families or friends together. A school janitor reframes his work as helping children learn by providing them with a safe environment. A garbage collector takes pride in keeping his city clean and disease-free. An administrative assistant understands that photocopying reports assists in disseminating information critical to decision making. All work has meaning.

Finding Meaning in the Meaningless. Think of the activities and tasks you do on a regular basis at home and work which, at first glance, seem to hold little value. What meaning can you associate with these tasks? Whom are they helping? How are you making a difference by completing them? How might you do this work differently to make it more meaningful? Would you feel different about what you were doing if you saw it as more meaningful?

Practice Positive Virtues

A fascinating body of research is emerging called "positive psychology." As a strength-based rather than deficit-based perspective, it fits in very well with the ideas this book is exploring. Thanks to this research, we now know about the powerful relationship between virtues like optimism, forgiveness, kindness and gratitude and a sense of well-being. We also know about the relationship between these qualities and spirit at work.

Choose Optimism

Do you constantly blame yourself for things that go wrong and believe that nothing good will come your way? Are you continually scanning for signs of danger? Or do you hold a world view that good things come your way? Are you on the lookout for the positive? Or do you need to be reminded frequently of the good things happening around you?

Which list below best fits how you see the world?

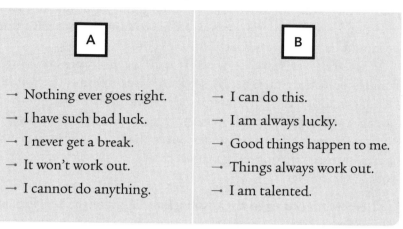

A	**B**
→ Nothing ever goes right.	→ I can do this.
→ I have such bad luck.	→ I am always lucky.
→ I never get a break.	→ Good things happen to me.
→ It won't work out.	→ Things always work out.
→ I cannot do anything.	→ I am talented.

If you chose column A, you are probably a pessimist and if you chose B, an optimist. Optimism is highly related to our sense of overall happiness, work performance and physical health. Did you know that optimistic men are half as likely to develop heart disease as pessimistic men?[28] I suspect being optimistic similarly benefits women.

Notice what you notice: Optimist or pessimist? Become a witness to your behaviors and thoughts. Listen for the words you use as you explain events or situations to others. In each of these examples, which statement sounds like something you would say?

- ↓ Do you give up easily? (I can't figure this out. My supervisor will have to get someone else to do it.) Or do you resist helplessness? (This is a tough one. I bet I can get someone to help me figure it out.)

- ↓ Do you speak about bad events in terms of "always" or "never"? (We always run out of money. We never have enough resources.) Or "sometimes" and "lately"? (Sometimes/lately we run short of money before the end of the month.)

- ↓ Do you generalize? (There is never enough money.) Or are you specific? (We knew that taking the trip was going to make us short on cash for a few months, but we felt it would be worth it.)

- Do you turn everything into a catastrophe? (You can't trust this company anymore.) Or isolate events? (Our boss made a bad decision last week.)

In the four examples above, the first statements are pessimistic and the second are optimistic. Can you identify the times you are optimistic and the times you are pessimistic?

Flip the switch: Tips to increase optimism. Our thoughts and beliefs influence the way we view the world, and they can be changed. Seligman, in *Learned Optimism,*[29] presents a well-documented method for building optimism — recognizing and then disputing pessimistic thoughts. Here are a few ideas you can begin to practice now:

- Be on the lookout for pessimistic thoughts.

- Immediately take action by arguing against pessimistic thoughts. Stand up to them the way you would stand up to someone who might inappropriately and negatively judge your child.

- Look for evidence that contradicts your thoughts (for example, point to the holes in your catastrophic explanation).

- Consider alternative explanations. This is not always easy, especially when our thoughts are entrenched. Look for ones that are specific, non-personal and that you can change. (For example, alternate explanations for being unsuccessful in a job interview might include: this particular interview was difficult (specific); the organization was looking for a different skill set than I have (non-personal); I didn't spend enough time researching the company (change).

- Put things into perspective. Just because you didn't do well in the interview does not mean you will never get a job.

- Ask, "How useful is this belief?" Is it serving me at this time? Can I let it go? Sometimes we have inherited these beliefs and unconsciously made them our own. Other times, it seems that holding onto the belief is more important than accepting the truth.

ᘐ Act with optimistic intent. What would it be like to be optimistic? What would it look like? How would you act? Start behaving in that way and you will soon notice that your switch has flipped.

Say Your Blessings: Express Gratitude and Thanksgiving

The ability to notice, appreciate and savor the elements of our life is an essential determinant of well-being.[30] Those of us who are grateful are happier, more hopeful and more helpful to others. We are less anxious, more spiritually inclined and report higher levels of well-being.[31] It is not surprising that people with spirit at work are grateful.

We are all familiar with the feeling of gratitude. Somebody does something nice for us or gives us a gift and we feel thankful. We know that they didn't have to make the gesture and that they did it for our benefit. We experience gratitude (and this is key) when we value the gift (material or, more often, non-material) and the intent of the person doing the deed. Too often, others are benevolent towards us but we are unaware of this or the value of the offering. We miss out on the feelings of gratitude and, of course, the benefits. The foundation of gratitude is knowing the gift was freely given, no strings attached. There is also awareness that we didn't do anything to deserve the gift.

But gratitude is more than the grateful response. It is also a sense of awe and wonder for life and a thankfulness for what we have. One day I struck up a conversation with an elderly woman as I waited for an eye exam. I was taken with her obvious vitality and zest for life and asked her about it. She said, at her age, the first thing she does in the morning is open the newspaper and read the obituary. When she sees that her name is not there, she says, "Yes! I have another day," and turns to the sports section. Now *that* is appreciation for life.

Gratitude is an approach to life — a way of thinking — that can be chosen freely. It is not dependent on wealth, occupation, position or health. We can choose gratitude even when we are unhappy with our work, colleagues or boss. We can choose gratitude when we feel stress. We can even choose gratitude when we are criticized and feel inadequate.

Although some of us are naturally more grateful than others, gratitude is something we can develop.[32] Let me tell you about some interesting research by psychologists Robert Emmons and Michael McCullough, leading American investigators of gratitude. During a ten-week study, they randomly assigned a large group of people into three groups. Every week, one group wrote down what they were grateful for, another wrote about hassles and the third wrote about neutral matters. At the end of the ten weeks, which group do you think felt better about their lives? Those who kept a gratitude journal not only felt more joy, happiness and satisfaction; they also exercised more, had fewer physical symptoms like headaches, stomach upset and muscle stiffness, and were more optimistic about the upcoming week than participants in the other two groups.

Writing a gratitude letter and making a gratitude visit to a person who has made a significant difference in your life, but whom you have never properly thanked, is another powerful way to increase your sense of well-being. One study showed that simply writing and delivering one letter increased happiness more than any other gratitude intervention. A single gratitude visit boosted happiness for one month, whereas additional gratitude visits increased happiness even after six months.

Practicing gratitude has a positive effect on both the person receiving it and the person expressing it. It is hard to be upset or negative when we are being thankful. Hans Selye,[33] often referred to as the "father of stress," contended that "among all emotions, there is one which, more than any other, accounts for the presence or absence of stress in human relations: that is the feeling of gratitude." What are you grateful for in your life? And whom are you grateful to? Have you told them? I invite you to write them a gratitude letter.

• • • • • • •

It is often easier to feel gratitude towards people in our personal lives, or things we have, than it is to be thankful for our work. Here are some tips for practicing gratitude at work:

- ☙ Express appreciation for employment.
- ☙ Give thanks for all that your work affords you (home, food, vacation).

- Instead of asking what didn't go well, ask what did go well and give thanks for that.
- Replace complaints with thoughts about what you are grateful for.
- Start a meeting with a moment of reflection for the "good things" that are happening at work.
- Thank your administrative support staff.
- Honor those who go the extra mile.
- Take the custodial staff for lunch.
- Write about aspects in your life for which you are grateful (at work and otherwise).
- Savor moments of success along the way.

Count Your Blessings

Choose a special notebook or a pad of paper that will be your Gratitude Journal. Every night, perhaps before or after you brush your teeth, set aside five minutes to be thankful. Reflect over that past twenty-four hours and write down, on separate lines, up to five things for which you are grateful. Try to choose ideas across all areas of your life. The elderly woman I met at the optometrist's office (the one who celebrates her obituary not being in that morning's paper) might create the following list:

1. I woke up this morning.
2. My favorite sports team is doing well.
3. I live in a country that has medical coverage.
4. My grandchildren came to visit.
5. I am still able to dance.

Maybe we're grateful simply for being able to take a fifteen-minute coffee break. What matters is that we are aware of being grateful and express it — even if just to ourselves. Once we open our heart to gratitude, we will increasingly begin to notice things we are grateful for, including work. So when the opportunity arises, pause and give thanks.

Pave the Road to Peace with Forgiveness

Forgiveness is something we do for ourselves — whether we are forgiving others or ourselves. It is a way to set ourselves free by relinquishing the hold that anger and resentment towards others, or guilt and shame we feel inside, has over us. Forgiving others or ourselves is a conscious choice: "I am not going to let this control me."

Whether we feel content and happy or bitter and dissatisfied about our past depends solely on our memories. That is why expressing gratitude is so effective in increasing our sense of well-being; it magnifies good memories from the past. In bringing attention to these positive thoughts, in essence, we are rewriting our past.

Forgiveness becomes another way to reshape our past. To forgive ourselves or someone else is to finish old business, and that allows us to experience the present. It means choosing to let go of angry thoughts and feelings associated with some perceived injustice. Unfortunately, it is not as easy to forgive as it is to express gratitude.

• • • • • • •

Here are a few reasons we continue to blame or punish rather than forgive ourselves:

- We do not want to forget the wrongdoing.
- We think that to forgive ourselves is to excuse our behavior.
- We believe that the guilt or shame we feel will prevent us from committing the transgression again.
- We think that it is only fair to continue to feel badly about what we did.
- We believe that it will help us make good decisions in the future.

Many of us find self-forgiveness more difficult than forgiving others. Forgiving ourselves has to do with accepting ourselves as human beings who make mistakes. It is about letting go of shame, guilt and anger towards ourselves for past errors. It is about understanding and grieving what we have done and then letting it go.

• • • • • • •

Steps to forgiving self include:

1. Experience the feelings (guilt, shame, regret) as you recall the event.

2. Acknowledge and accept responsibility for your wrongdoing.

3. Allow yourself to grieve.

4. Determine what you need to do to forgive yourself and follow through.

5. Where possible, repair the harm you have done.

6. Commit to forgiving yourself. Tell a friend or write in a journal. Forgive.

7. When feelings of guilt or shame arise, remind yourself that you have forgiven. Call your friend or reread your journal entry.

• • • • • • •

Reasons to continue holding onto our bitterness or grudge rather than forgive others are a little different. They include:

- We are afraid that forgiving will make us vulnerable to being hurt again and we want to protect ourselves.

- We feel that forgiving is choosing the offender over the victim and we want to honor the victim.

- We think that the act of forgiving perpetuates abuse.

- We want revenge — for the perpetrator to pay.

- We are waiting for an apology, for the perpetrator to take responsibility for what he or she has done.

- We believe that to forgive is to accept or excuse what happened, and we feel that we can never do that.

But forgiveness is not about accepting, condoning, excusing or forgetting. It is about releasing our shame and guilt or anger and resentment and being able to move on. Depending on the situation, we may never accept or excuse what happened. Nor is forgiveness about obstructing justice. We can forgive and see justice realized. Finally, forgiveness is not about forgetting. We will rarely forget the event. But upon forgiving, we may be able to release our deeply held resentment and recall the event in a new way.

Ready to forgive someone else? Everett Worthington,[34] the leading investigator on forgiveness, describes a five-step process he calls REACH. Although very effective, it is not always easy.

Here are the steps:

1. *Recall the hurt.* Be as objective as you can as you visualize the event.

2. *Empathize.* Try to understand the point of view of the person who hurt you. What might be her story?

3. *Give the altruistic gift of forgiveness.* Remember a time when you offended someone and were forgiven. Tell yourself that you can rise above the hurt and revenge. Visualize how it feels to be free from anger and resentment.

4. *Commit to forgive publicly.* Tell a friend, write a letter of forgiveness or write it in your journal.

5. *Hold onto forgiveness.* As memories of the event come up again, and they will, remind yourself that you have forgiven. Reread your forgiveness letter or diary. Release resentments and anger.

Here is the thought process an employee might go through after he is fired from his job at an automobile manufacturing plant.

1. The company was in trouble. Gas prices were soaring. The sales of SUVs plummeted. Many families chose to become a one-car family. Revenue was at an all-time low. The decision makers must have worried whether the company would go under.

2. The company had to make some cuts in order to survive. I can see how they decided to lay off some employees. It must have been a tough decision and even tougher for the managers to tell us. I can imagine

how hard it was to choose which of us would stay and which would go. I just wish I could have stayed. I have so many financial responsibilities. But how could they choose me — a guy with only three years of service — over a guy with twenty years of service?

3. I remember screwing up in my life and how people didn't hold it against me. They never forgot what I did, but they were able to move on. That sure felt good. I can do this. I mean, this resentment and anger isn't helping me any. I am ready to forgive.

4. I am going to call some of the other guys who were also let go and tell them that I am ready to let go of this and move on.

5. When I experience resentment again as I struggle financially or when I have difficulties finding another job, I can remind myself that I have let this go and am moving on.

Forgiveness is a choice. To hang onto resentment leads to stress, anxiety and even depression. When we forgive, we feel less anger, less stress and increased optimism. We experience better health. Forgiveness paves the road to peace.

On paving the road to peace. Who are you holding a grudge against? How is it serving you? What is standing in the way of forgiveness? What are the advantages of releasing your resentment? What would it take to release your resentment?

Commit to Courage

Courage is a universally admired virtue. Courage is the virtue about which stories are told, movies made and inspirational speeches written. Courage may be required to cultivate and maintain spirit at work. Or maybe being courageous results in that intrinsic reward necessary for spirit at work. Whatever the reason, people with spirit at work tend to be courageous.

Many definitions of courage abound, but I like the simple one offered by *Webster's New World Dictionary*:[35] Courage is a willingness to confront risk to do what one thinks is right. For an act to be courageous there must be an element of fear, risk or uncertainty.

Being courageous might mean taking action in spite of placing your physical well-being at risk, such as police officers, firefighters or social workers often do. It might involve taking a difficult or controversial stance, notwithstanding the result, as Al Gore did with climate change. Being courageous might mean following your heart, despite the naysayers, as many artists and musicians do. It might involve being true to yourself and maintaining your authenticity and integrity, regardless of consequence, as many people with spirit at work do.

Most of us have heard stories about courageous people like Rosa Parks, Nelson Mandela or Gandhi, but few of us have heard the remarkable story of Irena Sendlerowa.

Irena Sendlerowa[36] was a Polish social worker who saved 2,500 Jewish babies and children from the Nazi death camps during World War II. Working with the Warsaw health department, Ms. Sendlerowa had permission to enter the Warsaw ghetto, which had been set up in November 1940 to segregate the city's 380,000 Jews. Taking advantage of her position, she organized a small group of social workers to smuggle the children to safety.

Ms. Sendlerowa basically talked Jewish parents and grand-parents out of their children, saying that they all were going to die in the ghetto or in death camps if they remained. She and her team smuggled the children out by wheeling them out on trolleys in suitcases or boxes, taking them through sewer pipes or other underground passageways, hiding them in ambulances, or taking them through the old courtyard which led to non-Jewish areas.

She arranged for their placement into homes of Polish families or hid them in convents and orphanages on the condition they would be reunited with their families after the war. Irena made lists (writing them twice on cigarette papers) of the children's real names and put the lists in jars, then buried the jars in a garden so that someday she could dig them up and find the children to tell them of their true identity.

The Nazis captured her in 1943 and she was beaten severely — both her legs and arms were broken and she was sentenced to die. But the Polish underground bribed a guard to release her, and like the children she helped, Irena entered into hiding until the end of the war.

Once the war was over, the jars were dug up and handed over to Jewish authorities. Unfortunately, very few of the children's families were alive. Most of them had perished in concentration camps. Ms. Sendlerowa had been right.

Even though her work was remarkable, Ms. Sendlerowa's story was relatively unknown until a few years ago. That differs from the fame of German industrialist Oskar Schindler, who saved more than 1,200 Jews by employing them at his Krakow factory. A group of three grade nine students in Kansas researched Ms. Sendlerowa and her work as a class project in 1999. They wrote a play called *Life in a Jar* and delivered performances in Kansas, elsewhere in the U.S. and in Europe.

Not until 2001, when the students traveled to Warsaw, Poland, and met Irena Sendlerowa did her story became known. That's when the Polish press made this story international news — sixty years after it occurred. On March 14th, 2007, Irena Sendlerowa was nominated for a Nobel Peace Prize and honored as a national hero by the Polish parliament. Ninety-seven years of age, she insisted she did nothing special and was quite irritated by being called a hero. She said, "The opposite is true. I continue to have pangs of conscience that I did so little."

It takes courage to listen to and follow our heart, to stand up for what we believe in, to step out of our comfort zone and to take a risk. It takes courage to go inside and foster our spirit at work. As new employees, we often start with heart and develop courage along the way. The courageous heart is a very powerful place to be.

On being courageous at work. Take a moment to recall a time when your heart was courageous at work. Maybe you spoke your truth even though it was different from others'. Maybe you took a chance — a calculated risk — on a client, a patient, a customer or an idea. Perhaps you challenged the status quo. Maybe you risked your own vulnerability. Whatever it was, I invite you to remember the experience. How did it feel? What was it that helped you to be courageous? How might you use this knowledge in the future?

I bet you felt alive, energized, excited and inspired. You were probably a little scared, but did what you had to do anyway. You knew that you were making a difference. You knew that what you were doing mattered. This is spirit at work.

What's interesting about virtuous behaviors like courage, gratitude and forgiveness is that it doesn't matter where they occur. Whether it is with family, in our community or at work, the positive effect spreads across all aspects of our lives and impacts our spirit at work.

Reaching Beyond Ourselves

See Your Work as an Act of Service

It is not about me; it is about them — the customer, the client, the patient.

—Betty, business partner

We fulfill our deeper purpose by serving — serving others or serving a cause. It is through service that we make a contribution, and that is where meaning and fulfillment come from. As the saying goes, "It is through giving that we receive." Having spirit at work brings clarity about the focus of our work: "It is not about me. It is about the clients, the customers, my staff." It doesn't seem to matter whether we are a nurse, real estate agent, dentist, taxi driver or social worker; the view is the same: We are here to serve.

Service is a natural expression of spirituality. When we recognize our connection to others and become aware of our deeper purpose, we are naturally inspired to serve. This is the case whether we are doing manual labor, sales, service or administrative support — and whether we are providing a professional service, running a large corporation or saving lives. It is less about what we do than *how* we do it.

Seeing work as an act of service is more than providing good customer service. It is about intent and serving from the heart. It is about what we can do to make a difference for others, and not about personal or corporate gain. It is about doing our best, given the situation and resources.

Sheila was a graduate coordinator at a university. Among other responsibilities, she fulfilled the role of counselor to students. She dealt with students who ran out of money before their next loan was available, got kicked out of their apartment or ran out of food. Rather than be annoyed with the students, Sheila welcomed them. In fact, she looked forward to helping them. That was her job and she was there to serve. Sheila felt good about being able to help the students solve their problems. She took pride in helping them achieve their goals and was often invited to their graduation ceremonies. She knew she was making a difference. Sheila was very clear about her purpose — to serve.

Sheila's experience was different than her colleague's experience. Although they did the same work, Sheila had spirit at work; her colleague was struggling with burnout. What do you think was different? Sheila's co-worker was frustrated with the students and their lack of responsibility. She saw their visits as an interruption to her work rather than as a part of her job.

Often it is just a matter of our *attitude and thoughts,* because the work we are doing is already about service. However, if we do not see how we are serving others and do not take time to feel good about serving them, we lose most of the benefits. I want to repeat this because it is so important to our experience of spirit at work. If we do not see how we are serving others and do not take time to feel good about serving them, we lose most of the benefits.

To appreciate this point, we just need to think of someone who is a *martyr:* someone constantly doing for others while also constantly complaining. Generally, martyrs are not very happy, are they? Why do you think that is? They are not serving from the heart. They are just going through the motions. They are doing; they are not serving. Many of us are just doing and not serving at work. *Attitude is everything.*

When we feel good about helping others, our happiness increases. Once we realize that our work is an act of service and we are here to serve others, everything changes. It is not so much about what we do, but how we do it and how we view it.

On being of service. Who are you serving through your work? Who benefits from what you do every day? What would change if you saw your work as an act of service? For those of you in leadership positions, what would change if you began to serve your staff?

Plant Some Seeds

Even though we see our work as an act of service, we are not always in a position to see the results. Remember the professor who described her work as planting seeds? She didn't look for results; she knew seeds can take a long time to become fruit-bearing plants.

Maybe we can see ourselves as seed planters. We are connected with clients and customers, even staff, for such a short period. And yet the work we do will impact the rest of their lives. Sometimes we get to see the harvest, sometimes we get a little taste of the fruit, but regardless, we can know that the effort itself is worthwhile. Here is a poignant example.

Bob was an RCMP officer working in a small, rural town. One summer day, while on duty, he was called to the curling club to deal with an angry boy who was vandalizing the club with paint and ketchup. Tommy was a mess and acting out. He had been in trouble before, so Bob decided to take him down to the station to better understand why he was in trouble.

During the course of their conversation, he learned that it was Tommy's birthday that day, but his family had planned no birthday celebrations for him. As usual, the boy's mother had gone drinking. Tommy was angry. He had two dollars, just enough to buy a TV dinner, but no more. It was his birthday, and now he was in trouble with the law.

Bob called Social Services but knew it would take some time for a social worker to arrive. So he called his wife, told her the story and asked her to round up the kids in their neighborhood and organize a birthday party. His wife pulled together kids from a youth group she worked with. She got some hotdogs, found some gifts she had tucked away and planned a party.

When the boy came into the house, dirty and covered with paint and ketchup, Bob's wife looked him straight in the eye and said, "Happy birthday, Tommy." The boy began to cry. They found out later this was the first birthday party he had ever had.

The social worker found an older woman in the community who was willing to care for Tommy, and he stayed with her in foster care until adulthood. The police officer's family kept in touch with him until they were transferred about a year later.

Fast-forward fifteen years. Bob got a letter from the RCMP training academy inviting him to a graduation ceremony and asking him to present this young man's RCMP badge. Presenting the badge is the biggest honor a recruit can give someone; generally it's reserved for a father or special training officer. Bob was overwhelmed with emotion. He didn't even know that the young man had gone into the police force. He couldn't believe that this young man remembered him after so many years. Yet Tommy attributed his success to the actions of that RCMP officer many years before.

What I find remarkable about this story is that the police officer remembered the incident but had no idea how it had impacted the boy. That is the point. We hardly ever know, unless someone goes out of their way to tell us. And how often does that happen? The RCMP officer and his wife showed this boy another way of living. They planted seeds. Tommy learned about the kindness of strangers.

Can you think about a time you planted seeds? Or how you might use your work to plant seeds? Rather than looking for the harvest, celebrate the seeds you have planted. Know that once they are germinated, many will sprout, but in their own time.

The Ripple Effect of Kindness

Imagine if, over the next week, you were asked to engage in one pleasurable and one altruistic activity, and then write about the experience of each. You get to decide what is pleasurable (as long as the activity does not place you or others in danger). You also decide how you will be altruistic or kind. It doesn't matter whether the deed is big or small, or whether the person is aware or unaware of your good deed. Which activity do you think would bring you the most fulfillment?

Seligman had his students do this exercise. The results were life-changing.[37] The students found that the "afterglow" of the pleasurable activity paled in comparison to the long-term effects of the altruistic activity. Why? Seligman says that the act of kindness is not simply a "feel good" action, but a "gratification" that calls on our strengths to rise to the occasion. Perhaps this is why we hear stories about prominent and highly paid employees who leave prestigious positions to work in an area where they can help others, often at a far lower salary. That sense of gratification and fulfillment from helping others far outweighs the pleasure of money. The intrinsic reward of being kind is a key element of spirit at work.

We used to believe that only the person receiving the act of kindness was the one who benefited. Now we know that in addition to the person receiving the kindness, the person expressing kindness and anyone observing the act benefit in the same way. Scientific research has demonstrated that acts of kindness towards others result in a strengthened immune system and an increase in serotonin levels for both the person receiving and the person extending kindness. (Serotonin is that all-important substance that occurs naturally in our body and contributes to feelings of calm and peace. Antidepressants aim to stimulate the production of serotonin.) More surprising, the benefits extend to anyone witnessing the act of kindness. Hence, the "ripple effect of kindness."

A few years ago, I had the privilege of seeing this ripple effect unfold. My teenage son and I were doing fall cleanup and went to buy garbage bags. As we were standing in line to pay for them, I noticed an elderly woman waiting behind us. She had a large boxed artificial Christmas tree in her buggy. I leaned over to my son and said, "You know, Joey, it would be really nice if you offered to lift that big box out of the cart and put it on the counter." To which he replied, "Oh Mom, do I have to?" Joey is a really good kid, but he can be shy. I responded by saying, "Well, you know what you say about how adults view teenagers — this would be an opportunity to show them differently." He again said, "Oh Mom, don't make me do it." I shrugged my shoulders and said, "Well, it is up to you. You decide."

I looked ahead and saw a mom and a little girl. The girl, who was about three years old and sitting in the upper part of the shopping cart, faced us. The mom was taking items out of her cart to return them to the cashier. As she did, the cashier reduced the cost of her purchase. When I looked at what was being returned, I realized it was what she had hoped to buy for her little girl: orange juice, construction paper and crayons.

I immediately got a lump in my throat. In my previous role as a child protection worker, I would have given anything to see more moms like her thinking about their children's needs in this way. Uncharacteristically, I took out my wallet, found twenty dollars and passed it to the mom and said: "Will this help?"

She responded by saying that it wasn't necessary — that it would be okay. But I realized I was doing this for me as much as for her or her little girl. My heart felt so full. I told her it would mean a lot to me if she took the money, and she graciously agreed to. I cannot begin to tell you how good I felt as I saw her purchase those items.

What impacted me even more was the effect on my son. He turned around to the senior citizen and asked, "Would you like me to lift the heavy box onto the counter?"

So right there, in a period of less than five minutes, the ripple effect of kindness unfolded. It was like a little love-in. And the benefits didn't stop there. I am sure that that mom and the cashier told the story to their friends. I know that I tell it whenever I can, and I feel good all over again.

We never know when our act of kindness will have a profound effect. A smile, letting someone go ahead of us at the grocery till when they have just a few items, being present in the time we have with another person, making a phone call to check how someone is doing — these are simple but effective ways of touching another person's heart. Acts of kindness are definitely a pathway to spirit at work. So, go ahead and find a way to make someone's day, every day.

Recall a time of kindness. Recall a time when you a) experienced kindness, b) expressed kindness and c) witnessed kindness. How did each experience feel? What were the similarities?

Make someone's day. Make a list of ways you might be kind over the next week. Then choose one act of kindness each day. Notice how you feel as well as the reaction you get.

Here are a few simple ways to express kindness:

- Let someone go ahead of you.
- Greet the receptionist by name.
- Hold the door open.
- Pay for coffee for the next person in line.
- Smile at a stranger.
- Take a senior for lunch.
- Greet someone with kind words.

- Plug another person's parking meter.
- Pick up a piece of garbage in a public area and take it to the trash.
- Volunteer to help someone.
- Send a thank-you note.
- Offer the seat next to you to a stranger.
- Surprise someone with flowers, a fruit basket or a box of chocolates.
- Bring a coffee to a colleague who is working late.
- Send a birthday or anniversary card.
- Offer to take some of the load from a colleague or staff member.
- Listen, really listen to understand.
- Donate blood.
- Invite a new staff member for coffee.
- Ask your supervisor how you can help.
- Share a kindness story with others.
- Hold a kindness day at work.

Whether we are serving others through our work, planting seeds or getting involved in acts of kindness, the key is intent. Whatever we are doing, it must be for the higher good. One way to ensure we are working for the higher good is to connect with our source of guidance.

Connect with Your Source of Guidance

It is impossible to connect with our source of guidance when our minds are filled with chatter. Whether it is negative self-talk, a rehashing of an argument we had with our spouse, or a host of great ideas for our next project, we cannot hear our inner voice if our minds are constantly cluttered.

For example, it is difficult to discern whether what we are hearing is our intuitive self warning us of danger or if it is our ego bringing up unresolved fears. Is it that all-knowing part of ourselves that tells us it is time to find a new job, or is it just our ego looking for greener pastures? Was that our Higher Power trying to show us the way or another quick idea to pique our interest? It is difficult to know when our minds are not clear.

Take time to stop the chatter, every day. Go for a walk, meditate or listen to some relaxing music. Take breaks. Clear your mind. Get grounded. Find your centre. And then listen. Listen to your inner voice, that all-knowing part of you. Be open to your sources of guidance. We all have them.

Trust Your Intuition

Do you ever have a sense of what is needed without having all the details? Perhaps you have a hunch about which way to go when you are lost, a gut feeling that you ought to be doing something different than what you are doing, or a simple knowing of what is right for you, even though it flies in the face of all the facts? Sure you have. We all have. The question is: Did you honor the knowing or did you ignore it?

Intuition, that ability to discern the true nature of a person or situation, a sudden knowing of what to do, is a valuable source of information often ignored. But ignoring it can cost you your life, as Sandra, a police officer, found when she did not listen to her inner voice.

> In police work, it is so important to listen to your body, to listen to how you feel, what it is telling you. I am like a radio. I can tell what people are thinking or feeling, like "Leave me alone. I don't want to talk to you." I am also a little psychic. I can often tell something is going to happen before it happens. For example, when I got really hurt in October, my body was saying, "Don't get out of the car. It is not safe." I knew, and I was right. He tried to kill me. Listening to your intuition can save you.

Even though Sandra knew intuitively that it was not safe, she got out of the car and risked her life. Not only did she get seriously hurt physically, the experience temporarily damaged her confidence and the way she approached her work.

On being intuitive. Recall a time when you had a flash of brilliance, an insight into a difficult situation, or knowledge of what to do. What were you doing at the time? How did you know the information was coming from your intuitive self? Did you act on the information? What might you have done differently?

Be Open to Receiving Guidance

Miracles can happen when we are open to possibilities. Guidance and direction can come in a variety of forms, from deep within ourselves or as a supernatural phenomenon. The origin depends on our personal belief system. Do you receive guidance from a Higher Power or a Universal Source? Perhaps it is more of a natural tendency or instinct. Several examples follow that demonstrate how varied the experience is for people with spirit at work.

Earlier you read about how Karla's decision to go into landscape design was a defining moment. Remember how the sun shone through the window onto the ad of the landscape design program? Karla felt she had been guided to a career in landscape design. That was the only time she had seen the program advertised.

> I don't know that I have ever seen the program advertised again. Why they advertised it that year, I don't know. It wasn't a new program. It has been in place for twenty years, so I was surprised I hadn't heard about it before. I knew I was being guided and the ad in the paper was meant for me.

Even though she was convinced this was the career for her, Karla did a career investigation, learning everything she could about the program and career. She used all sources of information available to her.

Noreen, an educator, sees people as co-creators with God. She believes that although God works through people, each person has free will to do what they think is right. Noreen speaks about the relationship between spirit at work and her openness to receiving guidance from God:

> Where that guidance comes from is part of the mystery. I am convinced that spirit at work is part of God at work — whatever you call God, a Higher Being or Creator. Spark, passion comes from that mystery which is so hard to define. I think of it as God being part of us. I don't have an image of God as being a separate entity.

Kelly, the nurse turned organizational consultant, shares an example of how listening to her guidance prevented her from doing a lot of work for nothing.

> I have always followed my guidance since I was small, and that has made a huge difference. Some days, I basically follow my guidance from moment to moment. I wasn't always as conscious of it as I am now because I am working on it more. When I go to work in the morning sometimes I think, "Well, I should get on that project because it is due in a couple of days and it will be good to get a little further on." Yet my guidance will say, "No, no. Work on that project instead." I think, "Do that? Okay, I will trust you." And I go and do this other project. Then I get a phone call that alerts me that what I had been planning to work on would all have been for nothing, wasted. So this inner listening does make a huge difference to my spirit at work.

When they speak about receiving guidance, others refer to themselves as a conduit, recognizing their ability to receive and pass on an energy that contributes to the well-being of others. Rowena, the university professor, says, "We should open ourselves so that the energy can flow through us. We are a conduit. In other words, it doesn't come from us, necessarily."

Ben, the physiotherapist, has a different take on this. Listen to how he describes his work:

> What you bring to work is what is inside of you. It is your own life force, your energy. I believe that what I can do for somebody comes from inside of me. It is not a conscious thing. It is letting go of the brain and letting instinct work. Often when I am working, I am not thinking about what I am doing; I just do it. I ask questions and am interested in the circumstances, but the physical work I don't think about. I don't need my eyes. It is sometimes referred to as "bliss." You are conversing with the patient, but what you are actually doing comes naturally.

The common thread for people with spirit at work is their openness to receive and listen to such direction. Don't be surprised if people in your workplace don't talk about how they receive guidance or use intuition when making an important decision. Most of us are uncomfortable speaking about it. In fact, several people I interviewed had never mentioned it until I asked. When told that others spoke of being a conduit, they were surprised to hear that others used the term. Some saw it as an invitation to share their own view. Perhaps you can use some of these stories to start up a conversation with your colleagues. Who knows? You might be in for some interesting surprises.

• • • • • • •

What can do you to get in touch with your guidance?

1. Quiet the mind.
2. Give yourself opportunities to connect with nature.
3. Ask for guidance.
4. Listen.
5. Notice. Pay attention.
6. Record the messages/guidance you receive.

So the next time you have a flash of brilliance, an "aha!" moment, a simple knowing or a particular insight into human nature, stop and take notice. It is likely your personal source of guidance speaking to you.

Tips on Cultivating a Spiritual, Values-Based Life

1. Look for poetry in the everyday.
2. Find meaning in the seemingly meaningless.
3. Choose optimism.
4. Express gratitude and give thanks.
5. Write a gratitude letter.
6. Pave the road to peace with forgiveness.
7. Act on your courageous heart.
8. See your work as an act of service.
9. Take every opportunity to plant seeds.
10. Make someone's day through kindness.
11. Trust your intuition.
12. Connect with your source of guidance.

1. When was the last time you saw poetry in the everyday?

2. What is one task you do at work that at first seems meaningless, but on closer examination holds much meaning?

3. Would you describe yourself as an optimist or a pessimist? How is this serving you at work?

4. What are three things you are thankful for at work?

5. Is there anyone you might forgive, at work or elsewhere? What would change if you did?

6. What would you do if you were more courageous?

7. How is your work an act of service?

8. Where and how could you best plant seeds?

9. How can kindness change your workplace?

10. When have you used your intuition at work or received guidance on a work concern?

11. What one thing might you do differently? What would it take? (Record on page 197)

chapter eight

Refill Your Cup

How full is your cup? Full? Half? Quarter? Are you running on empty? Like a car, most people I talk to are constantly running out of gas. Even though we know the importance of taking care of ourselves, selfcare just doesn't seem to get to the top of the priority list.

How Are You Doing? A One-Minute Assessment

The oval below represents the "whole self." How well do you take care of, replenish and rejuvenate yourself physically (body), emotionally (heart), mentally (mind) and spiritually (connection with something larger than self)?

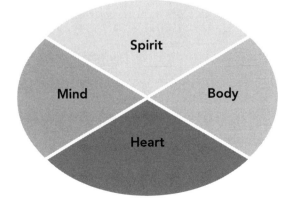

Do some areas receive more care than others? That is often the case. Many of us find that we focus more on one area than others. I like to work and learn, so my mind is continually stimulated. It is the other three areas to which I need to pay attention. What about you?

What things do you do to refill your cup — to replenish yourself? Do you make a conscious choice to take care of yourself or is it just an afterthought? For many of us, it gets no thought at all! Can you identify an activity that you do for each part? What are the areas about which you feel good? Are there areas that could use improvement?

• • • • • • •

This chapter provides several strategies to refill your cup and get you on your way to developing a plan that works for you. You may question the value of some of the strategies — maybe because they are simple or it is difficult to see how they may increase your sense of well-being and contribute to spirit at work. The activities that follow are behaviors in which people with spirit at work engage to keep their cup filled. Many are shown by recent research to improve a sense of well-being. But first, let's look at how we are doing collectively.

Where Are We At as a Society?

Turn on the news or open a newspaper and we quickly understand the impact of not taking care of ourselves. Take a look at recent media headlines and research findings:

- Employers identify work-related stress as the biggest threat to their employees' well-being, with more than seventy-eight percent reporting it as their "top health-risk concern."[38]
- Health costs linked to overwork and stress.[39]
- At any one time, between eight and ten percent of the workforce is off work on stress leave.[40]
- Of all disability insurance claims, thirty-five to fifty percent are stress-related.
- Job strain can contribute to heart attacks and strokes.[41]

- Employees who survive major job cuts are twice as likely to take sick leave. They also reflect a fivefold increase in backaches and muscle problems and are five times more likely to die from cardiovascular disease within the next four years than employees who work for companies who do not undergo major job loss.[42]

- Almost one-third of employees call themselves workaholics.[43]

- Workaholics are more likely to report fair or poor health, trouble sleeping and less satisfaction in life.

- About sixty percent of employees say they can't balance their jobs and family lives.[44]

- Forty-seven percent report they participate in "family time" (sharing a meal, doing things with their kids around the house or going out) only once a week.

- Twenty-seven percent say they "rarely" engage in these activities.

- Electronic dependence divorces individuals from family and society.[45]

Do any of these messages speak to you? Most of us are going faster and faster — in many cases, working harder — and our cup is getting emptier. It is very difficult, if not impossible, to feel energized by our work when we are running on empty. Even those who love their work feel depleted if they don't take time to replenish.

Some of you might be asking, "What about the company's or the organization's responsibility?" And you are absolutely right. As with the creation of spirit at work, employee health and well-being is a shared responsibility — shared between employer and employee. But what are you going to do if your company is not upholding its part of the deal? In the survey where more than seventy-eight percent of employers identified work-related stress as their "top health-risk concern," only thirty-two percent offered stress management programs to employees.[46] So yes, do what you can to make your employer accountable. At the same time, make self-care a priority. After all, you and your loved ones have the most to gain. So what can you do to look after yourself?

Be Good to Yourself

The best way to be good to ourselves is to take time for self-care. To be our own champion, the way we are for our children and friends. In a previous chapter I talked about how saying yes to one thing means saying no to another. Nowhere are competing values and priorities (see Chapter Six) more compelling than self-care. When we overextend ourselves and say yes to our boss, colleague, neighbor, friend or volunteer work, who are we saying no to? Our loved ones? Ourselves? The people we care most about typically get shortchanged. And we shortchange ourselves. So start by being good to yourself.

We know about the value of self-care. Yet many of us are challenged to find the time, energy or resources to care for ourselves. And we are not alone. Even patients told that their life depends on changing their lifestyle find it extremely difficult to change. In his book *Change or Die: The Three Keys to Change at Work and in Life*,[47] Alan Deutschman reports on the grim results of bypass grafts and angioplasties if patients do not embrace a healthier lifestyle. Although the operations relieve immediate patient pain, fewer than three percent prevent future heart attacks or prolong patient life. Why? Because nine out of ten patients do not change their lifestyle even though their doctors advised them they would die unless they quit smoking, quit drinking, changed their eating habits, exercised and reduced their stress. Two years post-surgery, only ten per cent of patients changed their lifestyle.

Knowledge and fear do not motivate most of us to take care of ourselves. If it did, our cups would be full! We need to become inspired from within to set self-care as a priority.

How can we become inspired to take action to replenish ourselves?

1. Say yes to self care. Affirm yourself and your value. You are worthy and deserving of self-care regardless of what else is going on in your life.

2. Assess your competing values and priorities and, if you choose to retain them, create a plan to integrate them into your life.

3. Create hope. Believe that you can do this and expect that wonderful things will happen as a result.

4. Set goals. Write them down. Make them visible. Share them with others. Refer to them daily.

5. Connect with the emotional results of your goals and with taking care of yourself. Feel the joy of connecting with friends and family. Savor the memories of taking a family holiday. Feel your body when it is pain-free. Relish the freedom of a stress-free weekend. Hold these feelings ever present in your mind as a reminder of what can be yours.

6. Surround yourself with like-minded people. Walk with a friend. Join a group. Sign up for a class. Start a support group at work.

7. Develop new skills to support your goals. Learn a new hobby. Discover relaxation methods. Try new recipes.

8. Get a coach or mentor. Find someone to help you learn new strategies and stay on track.

9. Practice, practice, practice.

10. Be gentle with yourself. Expect that you will slip and fall back into your old habits. That is normal when you try new things. Do not berate yourself, or when you do, reconnect with the emotional results, call a friend or coach, and start again.

Disengage

Research shows that far too many of us are disengaged from our work, which is not good for our spirit. At the same time, I am suggesting that we become disengaged in order to refill our cups. Sounds confusing, doesn't it? Doesn't becoming engaged in our work lead to spirit at work? Yes, but there is a difference between being engaged and being "always on." While being engaged is intrinsically rewarding and helps to refill our cups, being "on" all the time is draining and and depletes our cups. There's a negative impact to not taking breaks and holidays, even if we have spirit at work. The impact is greater when we struggle with work.

Drop a Few Plates

To get to the heart of what matters, you tackled several exercises and opportunities for reflection in Chapter Six. You became clearer about what is important to you, your values and your purpose. You did an alignment check on how well you are living in congruence with what you say matters. You focused on how to live purposefully and consciously and, as Stephen Covey[48] says, "Do first things first."

Now I am asking you to drop a few plates. Let go of the things that really don't matter. How? Ask yourself, "How important will this be in a week, a month, a year, ten years?" Will you say on your deathbed, "I wish I had done more housework, worked longer hours, written a better report or had a nicer yard?" Let it go. In these areas, strive for eighty or ninety percent. Let unnecessary matters go completely.

This is difficult, especially for those of us taught to do our best at all costs. Perfectionism can be our enemy and it is something I struggle with continually. Last summer when my husband and son went on a father-son bonding trip, I went to our cabin to write. My son had taught me how to text messages so that we could stay in touch. But as I wrote my messages, I was surprised at my perfectionism. I felt an obsessive need for correct spelling, proper punctuation and complete sentences. Did it really matter? No. Did my son care? No. Were imperfect messages understood? Yes. So what was the problem? I was glad they were gone for two weeks so I had some time to practice being imperfect.

We cannot take on ever more responsibility without letting something go. Each time we say yes to something new, we must ensure we consciously let something else go. Being intentional is key. Many of us live such full lives that there is no room to take on something else. So to manage, we often unconsciously let things go or just never get to the new responsibility. Perhaps this is how you have been managing. Do you then feel guilty about not meeting deadlines or fulfilling commitments? Be intentional about where you place your time and energy. Drop a few plates.

Reduce Hours of Work

The more hours we work, the greater is our risk for hypertension.[49] Researchers in California found that people working forty to fifty hours a week were seventeen percent more likely to report hypertension than those working eleven to thirty-nine hours a week. Those who worked more than fifty-one hours a week were thirty percent more likely. Why? Probably because working longer hours means making do with less sleep, poor eating habits, less exercise and more psychosocial strain.

In Canada, one-quarter of employees work more than fifty hours per week,[50] increasing their risk for hypertension by thirty percent. How many hours do you work? What is your risk for hypertension? Where can you shave off a few hours? Sometimes work demands seem to make working less impossible. Nevertheless, find a way to carve out time for yourself. Resist working late on Friday. Refuse to work one day on the weekend. Declare these as work-free times. Then refill your cup.

Unplug

One way to work less is to unplug. Most of us have a difficult time turning off our cell phones, email and BlackBerries when we are not at work. We are so used to working that we no longer know how to unplug. We put in an extra hour after dinner or after we put the kids to bed. We check our emails before we go to bed or during the weekend. Many of us wear our BlackBerries 24/7 — as if they were an appendage. Is this what the job demands? Or do we just want to stay connected? Maybe we fear our employers will overlook us or regard us as uncommitted. Maybe we are addicted.

Whatever the reason, being continuously plugged in is taking its toll. In an earlier chapter, I mentioned how the body fails to distinguish between a thought and a real situation. It may respond to worries and fears of imagined situations as if they were real. It may respond similarly when we are expecting something to happen. For example, when we are on call, even if we never receive a call, our body remains in "ready" mode the entire time. When we are plugged in, our body anticipates something happening. It cannot relax and rejuvenate.

A federal government deputy minister recently issued a "BlackBerry Blackout" directive that asked employees to turn off their BlackBerries between seven at night and seven in the morning. He requested that they not answer them during meetings and turn then off on weekends and holidays. He named work/life quality as a priority because he said achieving it benefited employees and the organization. When we can balance work and personal responsibilities, we perform more effectively as a team, and we do better at attracting and retaining employees, he emphasized.[51]

Fifty-seven percent of people work by email and phone while on holidays, according to a job-search website survey.[52] This has become such an issue that The Fairmont Hotel and Resorts recently launched an "electronic rehab getaway" at four of its high-end resorts in the Canadian Rockies. As part of the "digital detox," clients hand over their cell phones, BlackBerries, iPhones and other mobile devices, which staff then lock up in the hotel safe. After guests sign a waiver agreeing to go off-line for the duration of their stay, they are treated to such options as a massage, a hike, fresh fruit, herbal teas, fitness classes, etc. Packages start at around $500 a night.

Not all of us will get a memo from our bosses telling us to unplug. Few of us will ever get an opportunity to detox in the glorious Rocky Mountains. But it's still sage advice we can follow on our own. So let's go ahead and unplug. And during our free time, plan our own digital detox weekend.

Book That Vacation

Want to live longer? Take a vacation. In a nine-year study of 12,000 American men ages thirty-five to fifty-seven, scientists found that those who took yearly vacations reduced their overall risk of death by about twenty percent and their risk of death from heart disease by as much as thirty percent.[53] Women between the ages of forty-five and sixty-five who took frequent vacations saw their risk of death cut by half.[54] Now *that* is an investment.

Vacations also enhance marital intimacy (just make sure to unplug), improve sleep, boost mood, reduce physical complaints and decrease fatigue. Given all this information, you would think that we would make taking a vacation a priority. Yet North Americans take an average of two weeks of annual vacation compared to Europeans' three to four weeks.

We are not machines that can keep on working. Our bodies and minds are meant to work and then rest. When we take time for holidays, we give our bodies and minds the break needed to heal and replenish.

Listen to Your Inner Voice

We each have the answers within. Yet, too often we seek the advice of friends, colleagues and experts. If we slow down and take the time to listen to our inner voice — our intuition, our gut feelings, that all-knowing part of us — the right decisions come to us. If I asked you to stop, right now, and answer the question "What do I need to do to refill my cup?" I bet you could fire off a list within seconds.

We know what we need to do. We just need to quiet the mind so we can hear our inner voice. It can manifest itself as any of these:

- ⬇ a pit in our stomach that won't go away
- ⬇ a niggling thought that keeps coming back
- ⬇ a gut feeling
- ⬇ a simple knowing of what to do.

For effective self-care, we want to listen to our heart about what matters. Listening to our inner voice will tell us the steps we need to take. We also want to listen to our body about what it needs to feel replenished.

Listen to Your Body

Remember the mind-body connection? Our body responds to our thoughts. Similarly, what we do (or don't do) with our body influences our mind and sense of well-being. Taking care of our body leads to physical and mental health. What does your body need to be well? Is it crying out for rest, exercise, nourishment or touch? When we stop to listen, we know what we need. Here are three ways to renew our bodies on a daily basis: get some rest, take a grace note or simply take five minutes for ourself.

Get Some Rest

Are you getting enough sleep? How easy is it for you to fall asleep? Once asleep, do you stay asleep? One out of seven people has problems going to sleep or staying asleep.[55] If you are one of them, consider the stress in your life. Nearly one in four people whose days are stressful (either "quite a bit" or "extremely so," by their own description) reports insomnia. This is more than twice the proportion among people who report little or no chronic stress. The Better Sleep Council found that sixty-six percent of Americans blame their tossing and turning on stress.[56] Our bodies need rest in order to replenish. Sleep difficulties often indicate something else is going on. But you already knew that, didn't you?

Take a Grace Note

No matter how many demands we face, we are entitled to a "grace note," a period — I recommend at least fifteen minutes — we take for ourselves. In fact, as demands increase, so does the need for grace notes. We need to use that time in ways that are individually meaningful. Take a walk in nature, light a candle, listen to your favorite music, read, take a soothing bath, look at the stars or call a friend. What is important is consciously taking this time for ourselves, doing something that refills us. What can you do today to take a grace note?

Take Five

Feeling tense, too busy or stressed out? Take a five-minute grace note. Five minutes is plenty of time to make a shift, slow your breathing, lower your heart rate or gain perspective. Try these five ideas or create your own.

Get some air. At the first sign of feeling tired or overwhelmed, pause, consciously drop your shoulders and take a few deep clearing breaths. Take a walk. If you can, walk around the block or in your yard, feeling the air on your skin, listening to the birds, observing nature's changes and breathing in the scents of the season. All the while, feel gratitude for this time. You are sure to come back feeling refreshed.

Take a walking meditation. Alternatively, do a five-minute walking meditation, which contributes to good health. It revives muscles, stimulates circulation, aids digestion and minimizes sluggishness. It helps the mind focus and improves concentration. I like it because it is quick, I can do it anywhere and it focuses and quiets the mind. The instructions for a walking meditation are included in the guidebook.

Relax. At the first sign of muscle tension, give yourself five minutes to completely relax your body. Give extra attention to particular trouble spots.

Get to the heart of what matters. Create a vision board (like the one explained in Chapter Six) or an "awe wall" or a table or corner that can hold pictures, inspirational sayings, poems, photos or objects that represent what is important to you, what "feeds" you. Give it a prominent and accessible place. When you feel overwhelmed, take a moment, or five, to bask in the reminder of what really matters.

Go to the washroom. If you don't have an office to create the privacy you need, if nature is too far away or you fear that those around you will make fun of your efforts to relax, go to the washroom — with intent. Take the long way around. Walk slowly. Smile at those you pass on the way. Whether or not you need to use the facilities, sit and relax. Breathe. Think a pleasant thought. As you flush, visualize the stress being swept away. Feel the warm water on your hands as you wash. Take a little extra time to wash them. Separate from the stress as you walk out the door. No one will know the difference, but you will definitely feel it.

• • • • • • •

While I know that grace notes are not enough to keep a cup filled, they are enough to give a needed boost. Want to try one? Give yourself five minutes, right now, and see how different you feel. Taking the breaks we need greatly impacts our attitude, which of course influences our spirit at work. It is difficult to maintain a positive attitude when we are exhausted.

Mind Your Attitude

We can choose our attitude. We decide if the world is friendly or hostile. We select our perspective each time we are faced with a situation. We determine if we are going to be positive or negative, optimistic or pessimistic, calm or upset, happy or sad.

Although we may not be able to change the condition or situation that confronts us at home, work or elsewhere, we always get to choose our response. Minimally, we get to choose our attitude. Sometimes it seems there is little time between an experience and our response, but there is always a moment. And the choices we make play a key role in how we cope, how we are in the world and how we feel about our work. Our attitude is key to our experience of spirit at work.

Some of today's most exciting research involves positive psychology. Rather than focusing on ways to relieve suffering, scientists in this area are focusing on what Martin Seligman[57] calls the "good life." They are studying character strengths that help us thrive, qualities that make us happy, and activities that contribute to our sense of well-being.

Attitudes and activities that increase well-being and spirit at work are: positive thinking, living in the moment, optimism, gratitude, forgiveness, courage, service, kindness, happiness and hopefulness. You read about the first two in the chapter on living purposefully and consciously. The chapter on cultivating a spiritual, values-based life introduced the next six. Now we'll cover the last two in this chapter.

Be Happy

Do you remember the song "Don't Worry, Be Happy" by Bobby McFerrin? The lyrics implied that happiness was a choice and we could choose not to worry. I have to admit I wasn't too impressed when I first heard that song in 1988. It seemed so shallow, simple and unsophisticated.

So why am I promoting the concept today? Happy people tend to be healthier, more energetic, better at coping, more effective at work and of greater benefit to the people around them.[58] It feels good to be happy. The happiest college students are extroverted and have more friendships and relationship ties, even though they don't exercise more, aren't more religious and don't feel they have more good events in their lives than those who aren't as happy.[59] Increased happiness leads to more productivity and higher income. Happy people receive better evaluations and higher pay than those less happy.[60] I would argue that happy people have higher levels of spirit at work.

With an increased focus on positive psychology, researchers are discovering how to increase happiness and well-being. Until this research showed otherwise, many believed it was difficult if not impossible to change a person's level of happiness. Most believed that you were born with a certain level of happiness and that was what you had for life.

In *The How of Happiness: A Scientific Approach to Getting the Life You Want,*[61] psychologist Sonja Lyubomirsky reveals that genetics accounts for fifty percent of our happiness. Life circumstances or situations account for another ten percent. The latter include things we often associate with happiness: wealth, material possessions, living conditions, status, occupation, family relationships or belonging to certain groups. The remaining *forty percent* of our capacity is within our power to change — behaviors and thought patterns we can address directly with intentional action!

Lyubomirsky calls this the forty percent solution. She argues that it is more fruitful to focus on the forty percent involving our own behaviors and thoughts than it is to go after the ten percent associated with our life circumstances. To raise happiness, Lyubomirsky advises:

- practicing gratitude and positive thinking
- investing in social connections
- managing stress, hardship and trauma
- living in the present
- committing to goals and
- taking care of the body and soul.

Several of the recommendations coming out of Lyubomirsky's groundbreaking research are consistent with research findings about how to foster spirit at work. It doesn't matter where we practice these thoughts and new behaviors, because they impact us wherever we might be — at work, at home or in our community. What are you doing to contribute to your happiness? How happy are you at work? How hopeful are you about your happiness?

Be Hopeful

We tend to be more aware of the absence of hope than its presence. Many of us are inclined to describe a difficult situation as hopeless rather than looking for the hope in it. We might even be critical of others "hanging onto hope" and not facing reality.

Dr. Ronna Jevne, internationally recognized scholar and co-founder of the Hope Foundation in Edmonton, Alberta, Canada (the only center in the world dedicated to the study and enhancement of hope), thinks of hope as "the small voice in each of us that yearns to say 'yes' to life. If nurtured and strengthened, it invites, encourages, pulls, pushes, cajoles and seduces us to go forward. Hope is capable of changing lives. It enables a future in which individuals are willing to participate."[62]

What does hope look like to you? Sound like? Feel like? Taste like? Smell like? Most people relate to the following as signs of hope: spring, birth, a sunrise, a baby's laughter, running water, petting an animal, fresh strawberries, chocolate, baked bread and the smell after a rain. What is a sign of hope for you?

Being hopeful is often confused with being optimistic. Although they share similarities, they are different. Optimism is the expectation that good things will happen — whether or not we do something to make it so. It is a general view of the world. "Things will work out." Hope, on the other hand, is expecting our goals to be successful. It is envisioning a future in which we want to participate. "I hope to get a new job by the end of the year." Hope is not about wishing. As Wendy Edey[63] from the Hope Foundation says, "Wishing is best left for falling stars and birthday candles." Hope involves some activity on our part.

Most of us think there is nothing we can do to create hope, but that is simply not true. I suspect you have heard the phrase, "Where there is a will, there is a way." Researchers have proven what our parents knew all along. To hope is to have both the will and the way to pursue desired goals.[64] Once we have established goals, the next requirement is to have the goal-directed energy (will) and the planning (way) to meet the goals.

Why are we interested in increasing hope as a way to refill our cup and foster our spirit at work? Those who have higher hope

- score higher in satisfaction, self-esteem, optimism, meaning in life and happiness
- cope better with injuries, disease and physical pain
- perform better in sports
- excel in academics.[65]

Research on hope in sports and academics show that the results exceed expectations based on natural abilities. When they are hopeful, individuals do better than expected. Having hope does make a difference.

Create a symbol of hope. Today's demands make it far too easy to lose hope in our personal and work lives. A symbol of hope helps to counteract this. Choose something that represents hope. Maybe place a picture of a baby, sunset or waterfall nearby. Carry a rock or crystal in your pocket to remind you of your hope. Perhaps a recording of birds singing or a child laughing can play each time you turn on your computer. Select a screen saver depicting a peaceful place. You choose. Each time you see these symbols, pause and reflect on the hope in your life.

Raise a little hope. You can increase hope in the same way you can increase optimism.[66] Use the following tips to help set goals and find the will and the ways to achieve them.

1. **Set goals.**

   - Choose goals that matter.
   - Stretch yourself a little with each goal.
   - Write down your goals and share them with others.
   - Prioritize goals.
   - Choose markers of success along the way.
   - Carve out time to meet your goals.

2. **Find the way.**

   - Make several pathways to your goal and choose the one that fits best.
   - Break longer-term goals into manageable short-term goals.
   - Identify the steps you need to reach your goal.
   - If what you are doing isn't working, try another route.

3. **Sustain your willpower.**

   - Speak positively to and about yourself.
   - Plan for times when you get stuck or off track.
   - When you find yourself struggling, remember your successes.
   - Take care of yourself physically — get enough sleep, proper nutrition, exercise.
   - Celebrate your successes.

Take the Bite Out of Stress

Work-related stress is the biggest threat to employee well-being.[67] Many of us are sleep deprived and we blame our sleep difficulties on stress. Stress causes major health issues. It interferes with our relationships. And it negatively impacts our sense of spirit at work.

Because stress is so prevalent, most of us have accepted it as part of a normal life. We get used to the shallow breathing, tight muscles, and aches and pains. We accept sleep deficit and insomnia. Out-of-control feelings and a free-floating sense of urgency and panic are normal. We are used to constant fatigue and exhaustion, irritability and decreased or no sex drive. We are used to fast food, irregular meals and not eating with our family. We don't give a thought to being disconnected from others and not visiting with family members. We take muscle relaxants, antidepressants and painkillers all too regularly, or drink to chill out. We have become very accepting of the stress in our lives. And it is killing us.

What if I said, "There is no stress in the world"? Seriously, before you put this book down, think about it. When was the last time you saw or touched stress? You think you feel it, but do you really feel stress or do you feel your reaction to stressful thinking? It is our reactions to what we see, hear and experience that create the physical reactions — headaches, increased blood pressure, backaches, flushed cheeks and tension. Every time we are faced with a potential stress-producing situation, we get to decide how we will respond and ultimately what our experience will be. I know it is easier said than done, but not reacting negatively becomes easier with practice, and we soon see the benefits.

Several times each day we are faced with the decision, "Do I stay with these thoughts that produce this reaction or do I choose a different thought?" The choice is ours.

The top three things we can do to reduce feeling stressed are deep breathing (and meditation), muscle tensing and relaxing, and getting away from negative self-talk.

Breathe from the Belly

Less than ten percent of us breathe efficiently.[68] When we are stressed, we go into "stress breathing" mode and our breath becomes fast, shallow or irregular. We even tend to hold our breath. But when the breath is shallow or held, carbon dioxide in the blood rises. This throws the body into a mild state of alarm and encourages an adrenalin reaction that increases anxiety. This release of hormones makes it more difficult to concentrate, harder to remember things, and we become less agreeable. That is why it is never a good idea to argue with our boss, or spouse for that matter, when we are upset.

Frequent stress breathing increases heart rate, raises blood pressure, triggers anxiety and increases the risk of heart disease and stroke. Belly breathing, on the other hand, uses the diaphragm, which allows the body to take in the most oxygen and release the most carbon dioxide. When our breath is deep, long and slow, our body becomes more peaceful and relaxed. More than 1,000 studies show that belly breathing relieves anxiety, depression and chronic fatigue, without drugs. The effects are so powerful that the U.S. Food and Drug Administration has officially recognized breath training as a treatment for hypertension.

Belly breathing exercise. With a bit of practice, it is quite easy to learn how to belly breathe. Follow these simple instructions.

1. Sit quietly and observe your breath. Is it slow or fast? Deep or shallow? Regular or choppy? Do you breathe smoothly or hold your breath? Do not judge — just become aware.

2. Place your hands on your belly. Now take a deep breath and let it out with a slow sigh.

3. When you feel all the air gone, take another slow, deep breath through your nose. Feel your chest rise, then feel your diaphragm (between the breast bone and navel) and abdomen fill with air. Take note of how your belly feels.

4. Then slowly exhale your breath, starting from your belly and letting it escape up through your chest and out your mouth.

5. Continue to belly breathe until you feel a sense of calm and peace.

Breathing for the body-mind connection. Dr. Weil[69] suggests the following breath exercise to take advantage of the mind/body connection:

1. Place the tip of your tongue against the ridge behind and above your front teeth and keep it there through the whole exercise.

2. Exhale completely through your mouth, making a "whoosh" sound.

3. Inhale deeply and quietly through your nose to a count of four (with your mouth closed).

4. Hold your breath for a count of seven.

5. Exhale audibly through your mouth to a count of eight.

6. Repeat steps three, four and five for a total of four breaths.

Dr. Weil recommends doing no more than four breaths at a time for the first month of practice, but you can repeat the exercise as often as you wish. After a month, and if you are comfortable with it, increase the breaths from four to eight each time.

Meditate

Given the powerful effects of meditation, it is difficult to understand why more of us do not practice. Maybe we feel it takes too much time, think it is harder to do than it actually is or just think it is hokey. For whatever reason, most of us have not bought in. Yet.

Study after study demonstrates that meditation is associated with decreased heart rate, lowered blood pressure, reduced cholesterol and hardening of the arteries, slowed respiration, decreased levels of stress hormones and enhanced immune function. For example, a study published in the *American Journal of Cardiology* found that transcendental meditation reduces death rates by twenty-three percent, cardiovascular diseases by thirty percent and cancer by forty-nine percent.[70] Psychological benefits include reduced levels of anxiety and stress, decreased substance abuse and improved overall psychological health.

Scientists have known for some time about the powerful effects of meditation. But earlier studies were done with monks who spent a vast majority of their time meditating. Not very realistic for our lifestyle. Then research revealed that positive effects could be obtained by meditating for as little as twenty minutes a day. Now Dr. Judith Orloff, medical doctor, assistant clinical professor of psychiatry at UCLA and author of *Positive Energy*,[71] has shown that three minutes of meditation a day can reduce the stress hormones responsible for tense muscles and constricted blood vessels.

Who doesn't have three minutes? Given that we seem so pressed for time, maybe these quick time-outs, spread throughout the day, are the way to get many of us started. Obviously, the more often or longer we practice, the more benefits will accrue. But our focus at the moment is to begin. Here are two exercises to get started.

Quiet the mind (or basic meditation). Choose a place where you will not be interrupted. Again, if you are doing this at work or if you are a single parent, that might have to be the washroom.

1. Sit down and take a couple of deep, cleansing breaths — in through your nose, out through your mouth.

2. As you release your last cleansing breath, observe your belly fill up with air. Then let it out slowly. Go at your own pace. Do not try to control your breath or force it.

3. Begin to listen to your breath and observe the rise and fall of your chest. That is it. When thoughts enter your mind, just let them pass. If you like, imagine them encased in a cloud and watch them float away, or imagine them as birds flying overhead.

4. After three to five minutes, gently open your eyes and come back to the room feeling refreshed and ready for the task before you.

Visualization as a way to peace. Visualization is a technique whereby we envision what we desire. It's about finding a peaceful place (real or imaginary) where you can go (in your mind) when you need a break from stress. The basic meditation just described can easily be transformed into a visualization.

1. Once you have taken a few cleansing breaths and begun to feel your mind quiet, visualize a place where you have felt peaceful or calm. It might be a

special spot in nature — in the mountains, by a lake, in the meadows — or maybe it's a favorite vacation spot or secret hideaway. It might be a deep bubble bath.

2.   If nothing comes to mind, create it for yourself. Imagine what the most peaceful, loving place on earth would look like.

3.   Once you have your place in mind, take an imaginary walk. Look at all its beauty. Listen to the sounds. What can you smell? Remember what you felt like the last time you were there. Feel what it is like to be there now.

4.   Find a place to sit or lounge and take it all in. Allow yourself as much time as you need to feel peace.

5.   When you feel refreshed, allow yourself to come back slowly, knowing you can come to this special place any time.

Once you have practiced this a few times, you will be able to bring back the sensation and the calm, peaceful feelings with a few simple breaths.

Stress-inducing incidents are inevitable. Many of us are feeling an increase in stress at home, at work and in our communities. Regardless of where it stems from, the body always echoes it. Belly breathing, meditating and visualizing are powerful ways to reduce the negative impact and enhance our sense of well-being. The body does not know if our negative thoughts or worries are the real thing; thus it responds as if it were. The same thing happens when we meditate and visualize. The body responds positively as if what we are visualizing is really happening, thus making visualization an antidote to stress.

Muscle Tensing and Relaxing

Muscle tension is one of our biggest complaints, and the vast majority of us point to stress as the cause. That explains the increase in massage therapists, physiotherapists, chiropractors, acupuncturists and the like.

Where do you hold your tension? In your neck? Shoulders? Back? Stomach? Become aware of your "hot spots," and when you notice yourself holding tension there, take a deep breath and let the tension go as you exhale. Sometimes it is simply a matter of releasing — like we do when we become aware of holding our shoulders up to our ears. That is a pretty easy way to let go. At other times, it seems like our muscles have lost their memory for what it feels like to be relaxed, making it extremely difficult to release. In that case, go through your body and tense each muscle, then let it go. I find the following tension releasing process easiest to do when I am lying down.

Let it go: Release the tension.

1. Get yourself in a comfortable position, preferably lying down.
2. Take a couple of deep, cleansing breaths.
3. Begin to do some slow, deep breathing from your belly. Focus on continuing to breathe gently and deeply as you go through the next moves.
4. When you are ready, tense your feet, squeeze them tight, hold for three seconds and let go.
5. Tense your calf muscles, hold them tight, then let go.
6. Hold your quads, let them go. Give your legs a gentle shake.
7. Tighten your stomach muscles, hold it and release.
8. Tighten your chest, release.
9. Tense your buttocks, hold them and release.
10. Tighten and release the muscles in your lower back, then your middle back and then upper. Pay attention to your trouble areas.
11. Tense your shoulders and release.
12. Tighten your arms — first your upper arms and then your forearms. Relax.
13. Make a fist. Let go. Shake your whole arm gently.
14. Tighten your neck. Let go.
15. Make a prune face. Squeeze it tightly. Hold it. Release.
16. Stick your tongue out. Hold it. Relax.

17. Close your eyes and frown deeply. Release.

18. Tighten your head, then let go.

19. Take a few clearing breaths and release any leftover stress.

20. If you are awake (I usually fall asleep way before this point), draw your awareness to what it feels like to have a body without tension.

Letting Go: Out with Negative Self-Talk

Often, we are our own worst enemy. Many of us would never tolerate a boss or colleague speaking to us poorly or running us down, yet we constantly do it to ourselves. How can we feel good about who we are and what we are doing with thoughts like "I sure messed up that contract," "What an idiot I am," "I can't do that," "Don't be so stupid"? It is impossible. Even if we do a good job, help someone out or make a contribution, with thoughts like that, we are unable to experience the rewards.

We know about the power of thought and how our body does not know the difference between a thought and the real thing. We also know we have up to 65,000 thoughts a day and the majority of them are negative. Much of the negativity is about ourselves. It is called "negative self-talk."

Whether negative self-talk stems from our childhood, low self esteem or another source, we can stop it. With practice, persistence and patience, we can halt negative thoughts and replace them with positive ones.

Seven Steps to Positive Self-Thoughts

1. Become a witness to your thoughts and words. For as long as it takes to be clear about how you think and particularly how you think about yourself, observe and become aware of your thoughts. What is your ratio of negative thoughts to positive thoughts?

2. Choose your thoughts and words. Practice thinking positively about yourself. Because our speech is slower than our thoughts, it is often easier to edit speech than thoughts. Choose positive words.

3. _Stop it in its tracks_. As soon as you become aware of the negative thought, stop it. Even if you have completed the thought or your thought is half complete, stop it. Say something like "That is a negative thought and I am not having them anymore," "Erase," "I take that back." When she wants to change a behavior, a friend of mine chooses to wear an elastic band on her wrist, first as a reminder of something she wishes to change and secondly, as a source of behavior modification. To reduce negative self-talk, each time she observes such thoughts, she snaps the elastic on her wrist.

4. _Refute the thought_. Argue the thought. Give examples that show that the negative thought is not true. Say something like "That is not true. I am not an idiot. I just slept in this morning because my alarm wasn't set properly. Tonight, I will be more careful and as a safety guard, I will set two alarms."

5. _Replace your negative thoughts with positive ones_. Negate the impact of the negative thought by putting a positive thought in its place.

6. _Flood your mind with positive thoughts_. Take advantage of the fact that the brain does not know the difference between a real circumstance and an imagined thought. Positive thoughts have the same effect as positive experiences. Visualize positive outcomes. See changed behaviors. Think positive.

7. _Practice positive affirmations_. An affirmation is a positive thought or statement you repeat to yourself and implant in your inner consciousness as a source of inspiration for present and future actions. By using the power of affirmations, you state what you want to be true in your life. All affirmations are in the present tense. "I am accepted at work." "I am worthy." Consider your negative self-talk statements and choose the one that most resonates with you, then turn it into a positive statement. For example, if your negative thought was "I am useless," your affirmation might be "I am capable."

Create and Maintain Strong Friendships

Once again, science is finally learning what women have long known: Strong friendships can boost the spirit and health. These strong connections may well explain why women, on average, live longer than men. Women are more social than men in the way they cope with stress. Men are more likely to react to stress with "fight or flight" — with aggression or withdrawal. While aggression and withdrawal take a physiological toll, friendship brings comfort that takes the edge off the ill effects of stress. Shelly Taylor,[72] author of *The Tending Instinct* and a social neuroscientist at the University of California, says that this difference alone contributes to the gender difference in longevity.

Men and women who are lonely die earlier, get sick more often and have greater difficulty weathering transitions than those who say they have a support network of friends or family. Having a strong network of friends seems to help seniors live longer — more so, even, than having relatives, children or a close confidant. Want to live longer so you can enjoy retirement in good health? Take care of your friends today.

Follow Your Heart

What moves you, gets you up in the morning and keeps you going? Do more of it. Those are the rocks we spoke of earlier — the stuff that matters. And that is where the fulfillment, satisfaction and energy come from. It is when we take intrinsically rewarding action that it doesn't feel like work. This is when people say, "I'm doing what I love and I get paid for it."

Take time to know what matters to you — what is important — and do that first. The energy and fulfillment that result will carry you through less rewarding moments.

What Makes It a Good Day?

Don't know what matters or what is intrinsically rewarding for you? Answer the question "What makes it a good day?" As a prompt, ask yourself, "What am I looking forward to on my way to work?" "When I leave work thinking 'That was a good day,' what made it a good day?" Then look for opportunities to bring more of that into your work life.

People with spirit at work know what makes a good day. They know what gives them that intrinsic reward and keeps them going. This is what Ben, the physiotherapist, had to say:

A good day at work is when I get good feedback from the people I am working on. The momentum grows and carries from one person to the next, so it feeds me as I go through the day. It motivates me to be proactive, and to help others with the same kind of enthusiasm.

At the end of the day, I can say, "Yes, that was a good day." Busy or not busy is irrelevant. When I first started, I used to think, "If I can help one person today, I am doing what I am supposed to." Now my expectations are a bit higher. I want to help everybody in some way. Over time, I have developed enough resources that I can. Even in difficult situations, I still think I can contribute and help.

What If We Could Put a Price on a Full Cup?

Nattavudh Powdthavee, a social economist at the British Institute of Education, has created financial equivalents for life's pains and pleasures. Recently published in the *Journal of Socio-Economics*,[73] the study drew from a survey of 10,000 Britons asked about their health, wealth and social relationships. Based on their responses, each was given a "life satisfaction score," with "one" being totally miserable and "seven" being euphoric. Using a method called "shadow pricing" (fancy statistical analysis), Powdthavee determined exactly how much extra money per year a person needed to move from one point to another on the scale. Here is what he found:

- ⬇ An improvement in health from "very poor" to "excellent" provides as much happiness as an extra $631,000 per year. By contrast, a decline in health from "excellent" to "poor" feels the same as a $480,000 financial loss.

- ⬇ Increasing time with friends and relatives from "once or twice a month" to "on most days" feels like getting a $179,000 raise, while talking more often to neighbors is worth the equivalent of about $79,000 extra per year.

- ⬇ Widowhood hits hard, at $421,000 a year in losses, while getting married provides the equivalent happiness of $105,000.

So it seems we *can* put a price on our sense of well-being. Can you imagine how affluent we would feel if we took the time to refill our cup?

Be a Catalyst for Change in Your Life

None of these facts and techniques have value unless we apply them. As the book *Change or Die*[74] pointed out, we choose whether to become the ten percent change that ensures a life of intent, or passively accept the ninety percent status quo even if it stands for ongoing turmoil. The power is within each of us to change.

Tips for Being a Catalyst for Change

1. Appreciate yourself. Affirm your worthiness, your strengths and your willingness to succeed.

2. Believe in your ability to change. Watch for any signs of self-sabotage. Replace limited thinking with new possibilities.

3. Be positive. Focus on what is good.

4. Develop a plan. Write it down. Share it with others.

5. Connect with and seek the support of like-minded people.

6. Be gentle with yourself. If you slip back into old habits, remember your goal, how it feels, and take action towards it.

7. Celebrate each success, regardless of how small.

8. Express gratitude. Gratitude forms a bridge between you and every possible channel of good in your life.

1. How full is your cup and how well do you keep it filled?

2. What could you do to disengage?

3. When you listen to your inner voice, what messages do you hear?

4. When you listen to your body, what is it telling you?

5. What are five ways you can "take five" for yourself?

6. Which of your thoughts win — positive or negative?

7. How can you increase the positive thoughts?

8. What strategies can you use to take the bite out of stress?

9. What can you do to create and maintain strong friendships?

10. What steps do you need to take to be a catalyst for change?

11. What one thing might you do differently? What would it take? (Record on page 197)

chapter nine

Call to Action

We know that results are more likely to happen when we

- ⬇ have a clear vision of where we want to go
- ⬇ feel an emotional connection to that vision
- ⬇ set our intent to reach the vision
- ⬇ write out goals and plans to achieve the goals
- ⬇ align our behavior with our intent
- ⬇ share our intent, goals and plans with others and
- ⬇ include some kind of accountability measure.

Take Action

Throughout this book, you have been encouraged to stop and think about your work. Exercises within each chapter helped you get to the heart of what matters. Perhaps you completed exercises in the accompanying guidebook. The reflection questions at the end of each chapter gave you an opportunity to pause and reflect. In the spirit-at-work planning sheet at the back of the book, you've written about what you can do to foster your spirit at work. Now it is time to pull all these thoughts together into an action plan.

I am sure you have many ideas of what you can do to cultivate and maintain your spirit at work. To which ones do you have an emotional connection? Which ones will move you forward differently than the others? Now is the time to focus on the actions that are key to achieving your vision.

Chapter Six talked about being bolder. About stepping up and stepping out. Taking action that is transformative. We tend to have an emotional connection to steps that are bold and transformative. The Ten Times Bolder exercise will help you to decide what you would do if you were ten times bolder.

Repeatedly, people in my workshops identify this exercise as one of the most powerful — as the one that stays with them over time — so I encourage you to complete it or simply reflect on the questions that follow.

If I were ten times bolder. What would you do if you were ten times bolder? What might you do right now? What would you do if you were ten times bolder at work? Would you take a course? Write a book? Forgive yourself or someone else? Ask for a raise? Tell someone you care? Change jobs? Stand up for your beliefs? If you were ten times bolder, what would you do? And what would it take?

• • • • • • •

Once people think about being bolder, they often get excited, energized and empowered to take action. Some have found the exercise potent enough to propel them into action. They just step out and do it. The rest of us usually need to put a few things in place before we make such a move. This requires letting go of other things to make room for the positive we wish to attract. As you develop your plan, think about what you no longer need, what you are doing or believing that no longer serves you. Begin to let them go.

Create a poster as a visible reminder of your goal, that which you wish to attract, and the things you are ready to let go. Once you identify key activities (bold or not) that will move you forward, commit to spirit at work and complete a Commitment to Spirit at Work agreement (page 188).

Making and Keeping Your Commitment

Even though we have honorable intentions, following through with commitments can be difficult. Documenting our commitment and plan is one of the best ways to ensure follow-through. While only ten percent of people write out their goals, ninety percent of those who do, achieve them. Making your commitment visible is a great reminder of what you said was important. Once you complete the agreement on the following page, post it where you will see it regularly.

Another powerful way to ensure that you meet your commitments is to contract with someone (or a group) who will help you keep them. Although a group or partner who shares a similar intent is preferable (for example, someone else working towards enhancing spirit at work), it is not necessary. Choose an "accountability partner" who will support you in achieving your goals and celebrating your success.

My Wish for You

We are co-creators of our lives and have the power within to create the kind of life we want. The kind of life we deserve. We can all have spirit at work. The key is doing what we love or loving what we do. So do work that you are passionate about and is congruent with your deeper meaning for being. Alternatively, rethink your current work and uncover its deeper meaning. My wish for you is that you

- see the beauty within and appreciate yourself
- get to know others and appreciate them
- make positive choices and live with conscious intent
- cultivate a spiritual, values-based life in all aspects of your life and
- honor yourself by taking time to refill your cup.

Making a Commitment to Spirit at Work

Step 1. Commitment

I, _____ , commit to:

- appreciating myself and others
- living purposefully and consciously
- cultivating a spiritual, values-based life and
- refilling my cup.

Step 2. Action

I will initiate two or more short-term **tangible actions** to increase my spirit at work:

1. _____
2. _____
3. _____

I will initiate two or more long-term **tangible actions** to increase my spirit at work:

1. _____
2. _____
3. _____

Step 3. Accountability

For the next _____ months, I will share my progress monthly with

my accountability partner, _____ .

_____   _____

Signature   Date

Notes

1   N. Twigg, D. Wyld, & G. Brown, G., "Quest for Fire: A Redefinition and Reconceptualization of Spirituality at Work," *Insights to a Changing World Journal* (2001). Retrieved April 27, 2001, from http://spiritatwork.com/uversity/Twigg%20Wild%20Brown.htm.

2   R. A. Emmons, *The Psychology of Ultimate Concerns: Motivation and Spirituality in Personality* (New York: Guilford, 1999).

3   I. Mitroff & E. Denton, "A Study of Spirituality in the Workplace," *Sloan Management Review,* 40, no. 4 (1999), p. 83.

4   R. McKnight, "Spirituality in the Workplace," in J. D. Adams (ed.), *Transforming Work* (Alexandria, VA: Miles River Press, 1984), p. 142.

5   J. E. Myers, "Wellness Throughout the Lifespan," *Guidepost* (May 1990), p. 11.

6   To learn more about the Five-Factor Model of Personality, see R. R. McCrae & P. T. Costa, *Personality in Adulthood: A Five-Factor Theory Perspective* (2nd ed.) (New York: Guilford Press, 2003).

7   R. L. Piedmont, "Does Spirituality Represent the Sixth Factor in Personality? Spiritual Transcendence and the Five-Factor Model," *Journal of Personality,* 67 (1999): 985–1013.

8   M. Sinetar, *Do What You Love, the Money Will Follow: Discovering Your Right Livelihood* (New York: Dell Publishing, 1989).

9   M. G. Adler & N. S. Fagley, "Appreciation: Individual Differences in Finding Value and Meaning as a Unique Predictor of Subjective Well-Being," *Journal of Personality,* 73, no. 10 (2005): 79–114.

10 Ibid.

11 Barbara Coloroso, *Kids Are Worth It! Giving Your Child the Gift of Inner*

Discipline (Toronto: Penguin Group Canada, 2003).

12　T. Alessandra & M. J. O'Connor, *The Platinum Rule: Discover the Four Basic Business Personalities and How They Can Lead You to Success* (New York: Grand Central Publishing, 1998).

13　Wayne Dyer, *The Power of Intention* (Carlsbad, CA: Hay House, 2004).

14　Thich Nhat Hanh, *The Miracle of Mindfulness* (Boston, MA: Beacon Press, 1999).

15　Milton Rokeach, *The Nature of Human Values* (New York: Free Press, 1973).

16　R. Kegan & L. L. Lahey, *How the Way We Talk Can Change the Way We Work* (San Francisco: Jossey-Bass, 2001).

17　B. Greyson, "Reduced Death Threat in Near-Death Experiencers," *Death Studies,* 16 (1992): 523–36.

18　L. B. Jones, *The Path: Creating Your Personal Mission Statement for Work and for Life* (New York: Hyperion, 1996).

19　D. Richards, *Is Your Genius at Work? Four Key Questions to Ask Before Your Next Career Move* (Mountain View, CA: Davies-Black, 2005).

20　G. T. Reker, "Theoretical Perspective, Dimensions, and Measurement of Existential Meaning," in G. T. Reker & K. Chamberlain (eds.), *Exploring Existential Meaning: Optimizing Human Development Across the Life Span* (Thousand Oaks, CA: Sage, 2000).

21　Louise Hay, *The Power Is Within You* (Carson, CA: Hay House, 2001).

22　V. Peale, *The Power of Positive Thought* (New York: Prentice-Hall, 1952).

23　V. Frankl, *Man's Search for Meaning: An Introduction to Logotherapy* (4th ed.) (Boston: Beacon Press, 1992).

24　G. Zukav, *Seat of the Soul* (New York: Simon & Schuster, 2003).

25　Ibid.

26   Peter Block, personal communication, April 2001.

27   R. Lewis, *Work as a Spiritual Practice: A Practical Buddhist Approach to Inner Growth and Satisfaction on the Job* (New York: Broadway Brooks, 1999).

28   L. MacDonald, *Learn to Be an Optimist: A Practical Guide to Achieving Happiness* (San Francisco: Chronicle Books, 2003).

29   M. E. P. Seligman, *Learned Optimism* (New York: Knopf, 1991).

30   R. A. Emmons & C. S. Shelton, "Gratitude and the Science of Positive Psychology," in C. R. Snyder & S. J. Lopez (eds.), *Handbook of Positive Psychology* (pp. 459-71) (New York: Oxford University Press, 2002).

31   R. A. Emmons & M. E. McCullough, "Counting Blessings vs. Burdens: Experimental Studies of Gratitude and Subjective Well-Being in Daily Life," *Journal of Personality and Social Psychology,* 84 (2003): 377-389.

32   Ibid.

33   H. Selye, *The Stress of Life* (New York: McGraw-Hill, 1956).

34   W. Worthington, *Five Steps to Forgiveness* (New York: Crown, 2001).

35   *Webster's New World Dictionary* (2nd concise ed.) (New York: Webster's New World, 1982).

36   For more information about Irena Sendlerowa (also known as Irena Sendler), go to *www.irenasendler.org.*

37   M. E. P. Seligman, *Authentic Happiness: Using the New Positive Psychology to Realize Your Potential for Lasting Fulfillment* (New York: Free Press, 2002).

38   Buffet & Co. Survey on Healthy Workplace Initiative, *Globe and Mail,* October 27, 2006.

39 L. Duxbury & C. Higgins, *Work-Life Balance in the New Millennium: Where Are We? Where Do We Need to Go?* (Ottawa: Carleton University School of Business, 2002).

40 For more information, go to Warren Shepell at www.shepellfgiservices.com/research/iresearch.asp.

41 Heart and Stroke Foundation.

42 M. Kivimaki, J. Vahtera, J. Pentti, & J. E. Ferrie, "Factors Underlying the Effect of Organisational Downsizing on Health of Employees: Longitudinal Cohort Study," *British Medical Journal*, 320 (2000): 971–75.

43 The 2005 General Social Survey, Statistics Canada.

44 L. Duxbury, C. Higgins, & D. Coghill, *Voices of Canadians: Seeking Work-Life Balance* (Ottawa: Human Resources Development Canada, 2003).

45 H. Menzies, *No Time: Stress and the Crisis of Modern Life* (Vancouver, BC: Douglas & McIntyre, 2005).

46 Buffet & Co. Survey.

47 A. Deutschman, *Change or Die: The Three Keys to Change at Work and in Life* (New York: HarperCollins, 2007).

48 S. Covey, A. R. Merill, & R. R. Merill, *First Things First: To Live, to Love, to Learn, to Leave a Legacy* (New York: Simon & Schuster, 1994).

49 H. Yang, P. L. Schnall, M. Jauregui, T. Su, & D. Baker, "Work Hours and Self-Reported Hypertension Among Working People in California," *Hypertension*, American Heart Association Journal, 48 (2006): 744–50.

50 Duxbury & Higgins, *Work-Life Balance*.

51 "BlackBerry Blackout: Message from the Deputy Minister to all CIC Employees," *Ottawa Citizen,* January 31, 2008, online at http://www.canada.com/ottawacitizen/story.html?id=00e90468-cdb5-4181-abc1-42b245334df2&k=50819.

52 "Vacationing Canadians Stay Connected to Work: Poll," *Working. Canada.com* (2008).

53 "Work, Vacations, and Retirement: Will They Affect Your Health?" *Harvard Men's Health Watch,* 10 (2006): 6–8.

54 Dr. Kay Judge & Dr. Maxine Barish-Wreden, "Plan a Getaway and Live Longer," *McClatchy News Services,* June 20, 2008.

55 Statistics Canada.

56 For more information, go to www.bettersleep.org/OnBetterSleep/stress_sleep.asp.

57 Martin Seligman is a psychologist and founding director of the Positive Psychology Center at the University of Pennsylvania.

58 For a full review, see S. Lyubomirsky, L. A. King, & E. Diener, "The Benefits of Frequent Positive Affect: Does Happiness Lead to Success?" *Psychological Bulletin, 131* (2005): 803–55.

59 Seligman, *Authentic Happiness.*

60 B. Staw, R. Sutton, & L. Pelled, "Employee Positive Emotion and Favourable Outcomes at the Workplace," *Organization Science,* 5 (1994): 51–71.

61 S. Lyubomirsky, *The How of Happiness: A Scientific Approach to Getting the Life You Want* (New York: Penguin Press, 2007).

62 R. Jevne, *Magnifying Hope: Shrinking Hopelessness* (Edmonton, AB: Hope Foundation, 2003).

63 Wendy Edey, Director of Counselling, Hope Foundation of Alberta,

keynote speaker at the Alberta College of Social Workers conference, March 15, 2008.

64 C. R. Snyder, C. Harris, J. R. Anderson, S. A. Holleran, L. M. Irving, S. T. Sigmon, L. Yoshinoubu, J. Gibb, C. Langelle, & P. Harney, "The Will and the Ways," *Journal of Personality and Social Psychology*, 60 (1991): 570–85.

65 C. R. Snyder (ed.), *Handbook of Hope: Theory, Measures, and Applications* (San Diego: Academic Press, 2000).

66 Snyder et al., "The Will and the Ways."

67 Buffet & Co. Survey.

68 I. Bacci, *Effortless Pain Relief: A Guide to Self-Healing from Chronic Pain* (New York: Free Press, 2007).

69 A. Weil, *Healthy Aging* (New York: Knopf, 2005).

70 R. H. Schneider, C. N. Alexander, F. Staggers, M. Rainforth, J. W. Salerno, A. Hartz, S. Arndt, V. A. Barnes, & S. A. Nidich, "Long-Term Effects of Stress Reduction on Mortality in Persons Over Fifty-five Years of Age with Systemic Hypertension," *American Journal of Cardiology*, 95, no. 9 (2005): 1060–64.

71 J. Orloff, MD, *Positive Energy: 10 Extraordinary Prescriptions for Transforming Fatigue, Stress and Fear into Vibrance, Strength and Love* (New York: Three Rivers Press, 2004).

72 S. Taylor, *The Tending Instinct* (New York: Henry Holt, 2002).

73 N. Powdthavee, "Putting a Price Tag on Friends, Relatives and Neighbours: Using Surveys of Life-Satisfaction to Value Social Relationships," *Journal of Socio-Economics*, 37, no. 4 (2008): 1459–80.

74 Deutschman, *Change or Die.*

We Would Love to Hear Your "Spirit At Work" Story

We are always looking for new stories that inspire others to discover or foster spirit at work. Stories may be used on our website or in print materials, presentations and future books.

Tell us about a time that you were excited, engaged and energized by your work. A time you knew you were making a difference. You felt a strong connection with others and shared a common purpose. It might have been a peak experience or it might have been a time when you felt that you were living out your deeper purpose at work. Alternatively, tell us about your organization or company and how it cultivates and maintains spirit at work.

We invite you to share your story by submitting it to Stories@ rethinkingyourwork.com. Be sure to include your full name, email address and phone number in case we need to contact you for further information, and so we can let you know if we are able to use your story. By submitting your story, you are giving Val Kinjerski and Kaizen Solutions permission to use it in the ways outlined above.

Working with Val Kinjerski

Interested in increasing engagement in your workplace? Improving employee retention? Helping employees to be more productive?

Val Kinjerski, PhD, inspires and fosters spirit at work and employee engagement by reigniting employees' love for their work. When employees are fully engaged in their work they have a sense of well-being, renewed enthusiasm for work and increased job satisfaction and commitment. Their organization experiences improved customer service, retention and productivity.

Through Kaizen Solutions for Human Services, Val helps employees tap into the power within to foster their spirit at work, and supports leaders and managers in creating the conditions that inspire spirit at work.

At Kaizen Solutions, we believe in the

- capacity of all individuals to experience fulfillment and meaning at work
- ability of employees and organizations to reinvent and transform
- power of spirit at work to generate positive results and
- strength of co-creation between employees and employers to achieve success.

• • • • • • •

For more information or to receive our newsletter or participate in our courses, please visit:

www.kaizensolutions.org
www.rethinkingyourwork.com

• • • • • • •

To have Dr. Kinjerski deliver your next keynote, presentation or workshop — or help transform your workplace — contact us at Val@kaizensolutions.org or info@rethinkingyourwork.com.

Planning for Spirit at Work

1. Appreciating self and others

What is one thing I can do?	What would it take?

2. Living a purposeful and meaningful life

What is one thing I can do?	What would it take?

3. Cultivating a spiritual, values-based life

What is one thing I can do?	What would it take?

4. Refilling my cup

What is one thing I can do?	What would it take?

About the Author

Val Kinjerski, PhD, is a leading authority in the field of employee engagement and on the topic of spirit at work. An inspirational speaker, consultant and writer, she helps companies and organizations increase employee retention and boost productivity by reigniting employees' love for their work.

Val's passion for spirit at work is contagious and builds on her long-standing concern about well-being in the workplace. Her work and research have been featured in the national press, presented at many national and international conferences, as well as published in numerous peer-reviewed journals. She has shown that spirit at work is not a pipe dream or the result of lucky circumstances. It is available to anyone; it can and should be fostered.

Based on her research and experience as a consultant, Val developed and tested the spirit-at-work program. She found that participation in the program leads to a profound sense of well-being, renewed enthusiasm for work and increased job satisfaction. In addition, previous experience with clients has shown that when teams or organizations come together to participate in the spirit-at-work program, morale picks up, commitment to one's work and organization increases, and teamwork improves. At the same time, absenteeism and turnover goes down. Simply by rethinking work.

Beyond her work, Val loves her family, the outdoors, gardening, cats and building things. She lives in St. Albert, Alberta, with her husband Fred and son Joey and enjoys spending time with her adult stepchildren Jeff and Sarah and their partners.

For more information about Val and her work, please visit www.kaizensolutions.org and www.rethinkingyourwork.com.

Start Rethinking Your Work Today to Enjoy a More Rewarding Tomorrow!

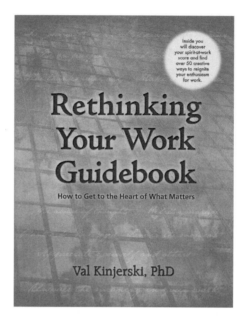

To start truly enjoying your work, first you need to do a little work! We can read all we want about rethinking our work, but the transformation comes in the doing. Thanks to this creative, practical guidebook, that's not as hard as it sounds. Its more than fifty simple, field-tested exercises carefully walk you through a radical "rethinking" of the work you do.

Research proves that by simply rethinking your work, you can have a profound sense of well-being, renewed enthusiasm for your work and increased job satisfaction. The clever and thought-provoking exercises in this accompanying guidebook will put you on the path to a more fulfilling work life today.

Rethinking Your Work and Rethinking Your Work Guidebook form a complete package for those who are wishing to enjoy their work and have a more rewarding tomorrow.

Order today from www.rethinkingyourwork.com